Dedication

This book is dedicated to the people along my life journey who:

Challenged and taught me difficult lessons
Listened and did not judge
Showed me kindness when it was most needed
Mentored and encouraged me
Helped me learn to trust myself
Believed in me when I didn't
Instilled patience when it was most needed
Gave me the gift of grace when I didn't deserve it

Without them, this book would not be possible.
Thank you!

Acknowledgements

My deep heartfelt gratitude goes to my husband and soulmate Philip who is my constant companion and always encourages my creative pursuits.

There are no words to express my loving gratitude and appreciation for Barbara Cook who sparked the inspiration for this book without realizing it. A heart and soul thank you to Carol Anderssen who provided priceless guidance for this book to become a reality. I also wish to thank Bethanny Gonzalez for her enthusiastic endorsement of this project. A special thanks to Raven Dodd for her expertise in the process of editing and publishing. Finally, I thank God who created me and gave me a unique set of gifts and talents to share with the world.

Introduction

Whether you are in high school, attending college or already working, this handbook will provide you with useful tips and skills for your life journey. College is not for everyone nor should it be. In today's business environment, especially with the advent of social media, high school graduates might feel pressured to pursue college. A college degree does not ensure success. For many, what is guaranteed after college is financial debt.

My desire to help others on their journey has been a constant in my life. This book is filled with valuable advice, numerous tips and ideas that save time and money. My purpose for writing this book is to provide a useful tool for young adults starting out on their life journey. *No one* can determine your future other than yourself. My intention is for you to learn many relevant life skills that you can use right now.

This life skills handbook shows the possible career paths that you might not have considered. You will learn how to create a resume that an employer would value and ways to distinguish yourself from the other candidates. It is also about learning what kind of questions to ask during a job interview. This book will show you how to set up a household budget, basic money management, time management and what questions to ask a prospective roommate. In addition, you'll find out what to look for in contracts before you sign on the dotted line and what you must know before purchasing a new or used car. You will understand what a FICO score is and why it is important. Much of the information you acquire from this handbook will be with you for a lifetime.

The goal of this book is to help you change and enhance your life as a young adult after high school graduation. Just because you graduated high school, it doesn't mean the learning stops. Life comes at you fast and hard. Situational awareness and learning to deal with blindsides can make your journey successful and fun. Difficult times will assist you in acquiring knowledge and wisdom that you will rely on in the future. My mother always said, "If you give it enough time, there is no wrong that in the end does not turn out right."

With faith, perseverance and determination, whatever it is that you set out to do, it's possible. Never forget that the people you meet along your journey can also provide valuable insights and lessons. Sometimes, it is not what you know but who you know and who you meet next.

"Whether you think you can, or you think you can't—you're right." Henry Ford

My Story

In reflecting on an old photo of myself as a young adult, shortly after my high school graduation, I recalled the sense of joy and freedom that filled my mind and spirit and most importantly, the sense that I could indeed accomplish anything I set out to do. I can still hear my mother say, "Nothing is impossible if you simply have the faith and belief that you can achieve it."

At that time, my greatest dreams and desires were to travel the world, learn about different cultures and experience all that life had to offer. Having traveled to 53 countries and five continents to date, lessons learned from those experiences have expanded my horizons. My career path was not traditional, as my journey included living in several different parts of this great and diverse country. There were times in my life when human resource professionals felt I was not the right fit. This was based on my average length of prior employments lasting only two to four years and the variety of career and industry choices I made. They claimed I moved around too much. Years later, the "moving around and variety of industries" proved to be enormously beneficial, as my employers found I was a quick learner and an adaptable employee. It was a blessing in disguise!

Some of the industries in my career path included aviation, the financial markets of Wall Street, media publishing, K–12 academics and higher education. Throughout my lifetime, I have been very passionate about every endeavor I embarked on.

It took ten years to complete my bachelor's degree in psychology and very soon after that, I chose to pursue a master's degree in counseling. My parents were also extremely proud of my accomplishments since I am the only one in my family to receive a master's degree.

Finally, I would like to share a story about instruction manuals. As young adults, you have grown up in a world of technology that moves at the speed of light. In most schools today, everyone has computers, smartphones, digital boards and other gadgets that make learning fun. There was a time when these computers and gadgets came with instruction manuals. It was necessary to read their manuals to figure out how to use them. Now, with so many updated generations of technology, it's not imperative to read through an instruction manual anymore, although sometimes necessary.

Have you ever read an instruction manual? By the way, when you were born, there was no "instruction manual" for your parents to read. In all likelihood, you arrived into the world, and your family was exuberant, joyful and elated at the beautiful baby that rocked their world. With no instruction manual, they had to figure out why you were crying; they had to figure things out along the way. After five years or so, they watched you go off to kindergarten on your own. For some parents, that separation was difficult.

Over the years, they have tried to provide what they thought was the best of everything for you. Your grandparents probably did the same thing for them. Ultimately, that is what most parents want for their kids. They want them to live a better life than they did. Whatever the circumstances you were born into, whoever raised you, please know that they did the very best they could to get you to this point in your life. Raising young adults is the most challenging job there is in the world today. Most parents and families think they are raising children when in fact, they are raising young adults. Isn't that what you are, a young adult?

Your life does not come with an instruction manual either. Once you are 18, your life and how you live it will be completely up to you with all the good and bad consequences. This life skills handbook provides necessary information critical for personal and professional success after high school and beyond. It is a book filled with *good to know stuff.* Learning never stops. When you stop learning is when you stop growing!

Contents

Chapter 1

College, Military or Vocational/Trade School

Many high school graduates are uncertain as to what higher education they would like to pursue. I was no different, since going to college was not a topic of discussion in my family. I must admit, more education at that time was not a priority for me, as my true desire then was to begin living my adult life. After working full-time with no satisfaction and wanting more out of life, I made the choice to give community college a chance. Next, my application to the local community college was reviewed, and I was accepted as a freshman. Excited to begin this new chapter in my life, I began my first semester taking the required courses. Towards the end of that first semester, my excitement and enthusiasm gradually diminished. Never one to back off a challenge or easily quit, I enrolled for the second semester. As time went on, pursuing an undefined education with no career direction was not for me. So, after attending a couple of semesters, I dropped out.

Another reason for dropping out was how lost I felt in a sea of students averaging one hundred per class. At this time, I concluded college was not for me. Anything remotely relating to the military was never a consideration, as it didn't appeal to me. Back then, vocational trade schools were not promoted as they are today as a means of making a solid income for life. Vocational training can lead to creating your own business, ultimately making you your own boss with unlimited financial possibilities.

College isn't right for every high school graduate, but it is the option most heavily marketed and promoted at the expense of technical schools, which offer career-specific training for well-paying jobs. On this YouTube link, career coach Dr. Marty Nemko talks about, "What Colleges and Graduate Schools Don't Want You to Know." www.YouTube.com/watch?v=xp6VR6tq9k4

When you graduate high school, there are many decisions and choices to be made. It is the beginning of making choices that will impact the rest of your life. Some graduates might feel ready to make these choices, and others are not ready to make what can be life-altering decisions. If you choose to attend college, pursue a career in any US military branch or attend a vocational or trade school, it is necessary to understand all the pros and cons of your decision. Up to this point in your life, most major decisions were probably made by your parents or in consultation with them. Now the choice is yours, and it is always a good idea to weigh all your options and consider the consequences.

Something to consider when choosing a college or university is whether the culture of the school reflects your values. Do you feel you will resonate with the professors and students? If you resonate with your environment, you will enjoy learning there, and you may find it easier to focus on your studies. At the same time, it is important to remember that diversity and different points of view will broaden your horizons and stimulate your mind. These choices are yours to make as you start your new adventure.

Attend College or University

The choice to attend college may be a widely discussed subject in your family or not at all. The decision to go to college is a big one. Like many things in life, there are advantages and disadvantages. Going to college costs tens of thousands of dollars, it requires a minimum of four years of school, and once you graduate, there are no guarantees that you will find the perfect job in your field of study. This can be true for many students who are unsure of what major to pursue in college. Sometimes graduates settle for a job simply because they must begin paying the bills. If you are pursuing a career as a doctor or a lawyer, then college is necessary. If you would like to pursue higher education, community colleges (also called junior colleges), can be an option too. Community colleges grant two-year degrees and are a more economical choice for students who do not wish to make a four-year financial and time commitment right out of high school.

Receiving a four-year bachelor's degree provides you with the ability to pursue graduate level studies that include a master's and then possibly a Ph.D. degree. There are also substantial positive impacts on short and long-term earnings and employment rates. One important consideration in pursuing a university degree is the chosen field of study. Some of the disadvantages to consider are that without scholarships or financial aid, you will have some level of debt, and the drop-out rate is high as the four-year commitment seems too long for some students. Additionally, there are no guarantees to find employment in your field of study.

During my lifetime, I have met people who studied medicine, and once they were out of school, they decided they did not want to practice medicine. The same is true for some who studied law, nursing and teaching. They pursued the careers because their parents wanted them to follow in their footsteps. Once out in the real working world, they realized their chosen field of study was not what they wanted to pursue as a career. If you are unsure of what you would like to do, it is best to explore your options.

A Military Career

Joining a branch of the military like the Army, Navy, Air Force, Marines or Coast Guard can be very honorable and prestigious. Both structure and discipline will be natural outcomes of a career in the military. The skills you learn while in the military will more than likely be with you for life.

There are questions that you should ask yourself before making the military commitment.

- Why do I want to join?
- Do I want to serve my country?
- Do I need a job?
- Am I making this choice for the college benefits?
- Do I want to travel around the world?
- Can I live with being told what to do?
- Can I live far away from family and friends?
- What will I do after my initial commitment is fulfilled?

These are valid questions that require your genuine and honest consideration. When you join any branch of the service, after you complete basic training, most of your immediate life decisions will be very important in determining which direction you follow. Understand that choosing a career in any branch of the military requires mental, physical and emotional toughness. It is not for everyone. Advantages include the honor and prestige of defending our country, the government pays for college, a guaranteed paycheck, training that will be with you for life, a military discount and the opportunity to travel. Some disadvantages for your consideration are that you simply cannot quit because you changed your mind, and you will likely be stationed far away from family and friends. Other disadvantages involve living with regulations, which means rules for everything such as getting permission for a tattoo, having curfews and working long hours, especially in the beginning.

Before signing up for the military, you must ask lots of questions so that you know what you are signing up for. If you consider joining the military, compile a list of questions to ask the recruiter. Develop your list of questions over time, not simply in one sitting. Perhaps ask some seasoned veterans what they wish they had known before joining the military. Ask yourself: Am I choosing the military because everyone in my family did it before me? Do I really want to join the Armed Forces? Learn to ask questions because the more you know, the better prepared you will be to make a life decision. This applies to all areas of your life.

Technical, Vocational or Trade School

Are there any differences? All three terms are interchangeable and describe a post-secondary education that is job focused and streamlined. These programs quickly and efficiently, often in a year or in 18 months, train you with the necessary job-related skills and background for a career in a wide range of industries. Today, many of these schools, in addition to their job-specific training, broaden the student's preparation to include more academics. Not enough high school graduates and young adults are considering these fields that might also lead to establishing your own business. Sometimes, people don't think about these professions as being worthy of pursuit. A technical certificate is equivalent to a two-year associate degree. Once out in the workplace, if you find the need for additional higher education to advance your career, the option is available. Vocational schools are an excellent alternative for you to consider.

Below is a broad list of industries to examine, and if you have an entrepreneurial spirit, it can one day lead to creating your own business.

- **Automotive**– a formal automotive education can open many doors, and trained technicians will always be needed. You can become a well-respected technician and work your way up the career ladder as a service department manager for a dealership.
- **Beauty**– a career in beauty can lead to various positions such as esthetician, make-up artist, nail technician, cosmetology instructor or even owning your own salon. Making people look and feel their best can be very gratifying.
- **Business**– a business education covers a large variety of positions that can include administrative

assistant, event management, accounting, real estate and office administrator. If you are interested in a business education, it is a starting point that leads to infinite possibilities.

- **Culinary Arts**– a passion for expressing yourself through food can open doors you never imagined. It is possible to find a job overseas in this field. Consider what food culture or ethnic focus will distinguish you from others upon graduation. Working in this career can have long hours.

- **Design & Arts**– this is another great career path for those with a creative flair and has lots of areas to explore. Graphic design, drafting, floral design, interior design and photography are just a few of the possible career choices for a creative mind.

- **Healthcare**– a career in healthcare offers flexibility because there are certificate programs that can help you move into the workforce quickly. Once employed, you may find areas of interest to further your education. If you simply love to help people, then this career path has many possibilities for you to explore.

- **Legal and Criminal Justice**– paralegals, court reporting, legal assisting, criminal investigations, law enforcement and forensic science are just a few of the areas that the justice career path offers.

- **Technology**– computer programming, information technology and cyber security are just a few of the programs available at tech schools to turn your enthusiasm into a stimulating career. There are endless opportunities to pursue in the technological sector.

- **Travel and Hospitality**– exciting and unlimited are the opportunities within this industry. Some of the market segments are hotel and restaurant management, travel agencies, airlines, resorts, cruise ships, casinos and private clubs.

- **Skilled Trades**– if you enjoy working with your hands, fixing problems and providing solutions, there are tremendous opportunities due to the shortage of qualified trade people such as electricians, plumbers, carpenters and gun-smiths. Flight training, HVAC, marine and watercraft repair, and welding are just a few of the skilled trades for you to consider.

Please note that I am not opposed to a four-year degree, rather I am simply making a strong case for an option that many young adults and high school seniors might overlook when deciding what to do after high school. One advantage of a technical trade school is job security since there is growing domestic demand for highly skilled trade people. In today's environment, skilled trade workers are disproportionately an older population creating increased opportunities for younger workers to fill their positions.

Whether you choose to attend college or a trade school, *make a commitment to yourself to complete your area of study.* Life happens to all of us, and the temptation to drop-out will always be right around the corner. Promise yourself that no matter what, you will achieve your goal. That was the promise I made to myself even though it took ten years to complete. Something always seemed to get in the way of completing my degree. There is great satisfaction when we achieve our goals no matter how small or large. Furthering your knowledge and education should be a lifelong goal and commitment.

Carmen Topper

Chapter 2

Finding a Job or Choosing a Career

We often hear the words job and career used interchangeably; however, they have different meanings. A job is typically something you do in the short term to earn money and can possibly turn into a career. Some drawbacks of this "job scenario" could include the lack of a stimulating environment hence poor motivation, boredom, no real mental challenge, a level of complacency and comfort. On the flip side, there may be no real stability leading to constant job changing.

In a recent conversation with a vice-president of a major bank, it was mentioned how some of today's young adults applying for employment are proficient in the tactics of interviewing, yet not proficient in actually being able to do the job once hired. They are well prepared and trained to answer all interview questions that indicate they are qualified for the position. Once they are hired, they lack the critical thinking and soft skills needed to carry out their responsibilities. In addition, the bank VP inferred that lots of today's young adults are just collecting a paycheck and not looking to develop a career.

A career-oriented position is probably best termed as a long-term pursuit of a lifelong ambition. Some jobs help people find their passion. I have known some very happy people who started a job at a grocery store and worked their way up, being promoted to department head and eventually becoming the store manager.

Many companies hire entry level positions. With dedication, hard work and company sponsored training, you can easily be promoted to a managerial position and grow within the company. In today's business environment, growing within a company does not mean a 20 to 30-year commitment as it was 50 years ago. With the advent of technology, the opportunities for well-prepared young adults are endless.

In the current business environment, long-term employment could be considered 10 years. The advantages and benefits are the ability to change roles within the company, thus acquiring seniority; pay increases and career stability. If your personal preferences lean toward structure, stability and routine, then looking to make a career out of a job is a positive direction for you. On the other hand, job hopping will give you more freedom, a new and exciting change of environment, different styles of peers and managers along with the possibility of more frequent pay raises. If you are someone who prefers independence, is a self-starter, likes change, is very adaptable and gets bored quickly, then the job-hopping route is a definite consideration for you.

Following is my recollection of how I stumbled upon my passion for travel, which ultimately led to an exciting career path across various industries.

My first job, while in high school, was working the counter at a neighborhood bakery. While still working there full-time after high school, a couple of friends mentioned an upcoming Christmas trip to Spain. They wanted to know if I was interested in meeting them in Madrid. I was, and with my savings, I was able to pay my own way. Since I was still living at home, the question was how to let my parents know of my intentions. Eventually, I figured out that purchasing a non-refundable ticket was the way to let them know, and that is exactly what I did. They were not happy and didn't approve of my trip since Christmas away from the family was unheard of and unacceptable. After much back and forth, they reluctantly gave in to my decision but refused to take me to the airport. This was my first time traveling to Europe, and I could hardly contain my excitement. In Madrid, I met up with my friends who had rented a car and thus began our adventure. On Christmas Day, I placed a collect call to my parents (a collect call back then meant the charges were reversed), but they did not accept my call. It had never occurred to me they would not accept my call, and for the first time in my life I felt all alone.

Actions have consequences, and I quickly realized that I have to be responsible for my actions. We continued our adventure driving through the southern half of Spain and typically spent two or three days in each town, staying in the inexpensive hostels in Toledo, Seville and Malaga. While driving late into the evening on our way to Barcelona, I looked up to the sky and was mesmerized by all the stars. It was then and still to this day the most spectacular evening sky I have ever seen in my life. Eventually, we arrived in Barcelona staying a few days and continued through Andorra with our ultimate destination being Venice, Italy. Driving through southern France, crossing into Monaco and then on into Italy at such a young and impressionable age, for me was a trip of a lifetime.

Disagreements, misunderstandings and differences of opinion about what to do led to several very uncomfortable situations. One evening, while eating in Milan, all the treasures we had purchased along the way in Spain and France were stolen from the trunk of our car. By this time, I was anxious to return home. Fast forward to my return home in late January; my parents were grateful I survived the trip. They imposed very strict rules that I had to live by under their roof, and to this day I am very grateful for their actions. Choosing not to spend Christmas with my family had consequences. Although I didn't like the new rules, the experience taught me accountability. Additionally, I learned that the differences and misunderstandings the four of us shared on our trip had a purpose. For me, it was lessons in tolerance and compromise.

My purpose for sharing this particular story is to give you an example of how sometimes in life we make choices that aren't thoroughly thought through. Every action has consequences, and the results being positive or negative are all part of our journey that will only help to expand our wisdom. With time, I realized that what I thought was wrong turned out well. As we traveled throughout Spain, France and northern Italy, I realized my passion for learning about different cultures and the experiences I gained were priceless. Although difficult at times, life presents constant opportunities. My passion for travel was ignited, and from then on, I made a conscious choice to pursue careers or jobs that included travel as a requirement.

So, whether you are looking for a job or a career, focus and preparation are the keys. Whatever it is that you are looking for, let's get started by preparing a resume. If you had a part-time job during high school and would like to find full-time employment, keep in mind that it will require a disciplined approach.

Do you have a Resume?

It was a difficult task for me to create my first resume since the only previous job I held was at a bakery. Think about it; customers walked into a shop filled with the wonderful aroma of bread and pastries, they placed their orders and paid. I used an old manual push key cash register and not the modern digital kind. I had to use my math skills to provide the appropriate change, and sometimes the bakery got very busy while I was the only one working the counter. When it was time for me to create my resume, I asked my brother for help, which came in the way of asking lots of questions. The more questions he asked, the more I realized I had in fact gained enough valuable experience to create an impressive resume. Multi-tasking along with stress management are essential life skills in achieving your goals.

Are you wondering whether you need a resume? Perhaps you have not worked or think the part-time job you currently have is not important. Think again. Whatever the circumstances, the answer is *yes* you need a resume. A resume provides the reader a summary of your skills, abilities and accomplishments. It is a snapshot of you. Some companies plan and schedule open house hiring events. The purpose of this event is to encourage prospective applicants to attend and apply for open positions. These events provide you the opportunity for a brief face to face interview that can lead to an invitation to return for another interview or being hired on the spot.

When attending a hiring event, it is extremely important to be prepared. This includes your attire and presentation. Without a resume in hand, you waste your time going to the event. These hiring events typically draw a large pool of applicants to choose from. When I scheduled open house hiring events, and the applicant did not have a resume, the interview was cut short. They simply were not prepared, and I did not have time to waste. In many cases, the applicants were not even prepared to provide a verbal summary of their skill set. A well thought out verbal summary of your skill set is essential for you to develop and can serve as a "skills selfie." Prospective employers must have a synopsis of your abilities, education and experiences. In the business world, employers are looking to fill a position with someone who offers the right kind of skills.

You may not know it, but you have more talent and skills than you realize.

- Did you participate in any clubs in high school?
- Did you work on the yearbook?
- Do you play a musical instrument?
- Did you collaborate on a school event?
- Do you know another language?
- Did you babysit children in your neighborhood?
- Did you provide pet sitting services?
- Did you mow the lawn for neighbors, or did you provide any other kind of services for others?
- Do you have technology skills?
- Can you figure things out?
- Do you like to read?
- What do you like to read about?
- Did you do any volunteer work?

These are closed questions designed to elicit short answers such as yes or no. The answers to all these questions will jumpstart the process to think deeply about what you have to offer a company. For example, if you are someone who can figure things out, look for ways to relate those skills to the position you are seeking. Figuring things out is about solving problems, so this particular skill is valuable to employers. You begin to create a resume that conveys your education, skill set and experiences. Get the idea?

Carmen Topper

Chapter 3

Resume Formats and References

The term "resume formats" was not in my vocabulary nor did I understand what the phrase meant. It took some time to figure out how best to highlight my accomplishments, experiences and skills on a resume. What is most important to remember about resume formats is the concept of being flexible and understanding what works best for you at present. Your career will develop and change over time. So, it is to your greatest advantage to be aware of and learn the most effective way to present yourself on paper.

Looking back through many of my career moves, using the chronological and functional formats worked best for me. Early in my life, I used the chronological format, since I held various kinds of jobs. Most young adults in their early work life bounce around trying different jobs to assess what fits best. In my case, I worked retail sales, became a legal secretary and did some modeling among other things. Later in my life, I used the functional format to emphasize the various kinds of skills and experiences I gained in a variety of jobs to demonstrate my adaptability. As my skills and experiences increased, my focus and efforts were to create an impressive resume using the functional format.

On one occasion, I used the targeted resume and landed the prized job. In this instance, it was necessary to highlight my experiences and skills, which were relevant to the position they were seeking to hire. In my own words, I mirrored the position requirements to my qualifications, education and career objectives. It's important to learn how best to highlight and distinguish your skills.

There once was a time in my career when I was responsible for posting job opportunities, interviewing candidates and hiring them. This opportunity provided significant insights into poorly written cover letters and resumes as well as very effective well written ones. The one thing in life you can control is the effort you put into things. So, the thought and effort you put into writing a cover letter and resume will undoubtedly shine through. It does not mean you will land the job; however, it can open the door for an interview.

When hiring managers post a job opening, they end up receiving hundreds of resumes. Hiring managers have their own systems on how to file all the resumes they receive. With so many resumes, usually, a quick glance of 15 to 20 seconds per individual is all that is given before consigning it to a pile. Generally, there are two piles, one for "pursue these applicants" and the second called "all others." Think of your resume as an advertisement. If the resume does not stand out to the viewer, which pile do you believe it ends up in? Your resume, when submitted online, is the first impression someone has of your overall communication skills, abilities and education. I will show you how to create a resume that stands out to hiring managers.

What are the different types of resumes? There are four types of resume formats: Chronological, Functional, Combination and Targeted. Each format is explained below and when it is best to use. For the purposes of this guide, I will focus on the more common chronological and functional resume formats. When providing your name, address, phone and email information, it is very important to include an email that is professional. Fancy names and nicknames are not appropriate, nor are they professional for a resume. My advice is to ensure you have a professional business email separate from the one used for friends and family. For example, yourname@gmail.com.

The **chronological resume** is the most commonly used format. It lists work history in chronological order, starting with the most current down to the oldest employment. A chronological format is best if you have a work history. If you have any volunteer experience, always include it as it adds another level of your knowledge. Also, this format is appropriate to use if your experience is aligned with the position you are seeking, and there are no lapses between jobs.

The **functional resume** focuses on your skills and experiences first and does not emphasize the dates you have worked. Employment history is secondary and is listed under the details of your skills. This format is best if you have lapses in employment, are in the middle of a career transition, are a recent graduate with limited work experience or have a diverse background with no clear career path. If you have specific skills with none or little work history, say a part-time job, then the functional format is the best fit for you.

The **combination resume** lets you detail both skills and experiences while providing a chronological listing of work history. This format offers an opportunity to detail your work experience and demonstrates to hiring managers your career evolution. It allows for the details of your work experience to tell a story.

The **targeted resume** focuses on a specific job opening and is written to highlight the specific experiences and skills relevant to the position. All your information including career objective, qualifications and educational experiences should mirror the position requirements. This format is appropriate once you acquire experience, skills and accomplishments in your work history.

On the following pages, you will find samples of the chronological and functional resumes.

Sample Chronological Resume

Mark Smith
1234 Homewood Drive, Any Town, USA 12345
Tel. (123) 456-7890
your.name@gmail.com

Education
USA Senior High School, class of 2016

Experience
Any Town Public Library – Homewood Branch
(July 2016 – present)

- Coordinated volunteer program "Story Time" for elementary and middle school students.
- Worked with front desk staff in customer service and sorted library materials appropriately.
- Organized card catalog to incorporate new materials.

Boys and Girls Club Homewood
Volunteer (January 2015 – present)

- Gained leadership and service experience through the Keystone program.
- Program focused on academic success, career exploration and community service.
- Tutored students to increase their Photoshop technical skills.

Activities
- Photography Club 2013 – 2016
- Illustration Club 2014 – 2016
- Economics Club 2016

References
Mr. John Connolly
Guidance Counselor 2013 – 2016
123-456-7890   John.smith@anytownhighschool.org

It is to your benefit if you can provide two or three references.

Sample Functional Resume

Maria Gonzalez – Customer Service/Retail
1234 Homewood Drive, Any Town, USA 12345
Tel. (123) 456-7890
your.name@gmail.com

USA Senior High School 2016 Graduate

SKILLS / KNOWLEDGE
• Research Skills
• Communication Skills
• Stage and Costume Design
• Microsoft Office Suite
• Typing
• Internet/E-mail
• Fluent Spanish (reading and writing)

ACHIEVEMENTS
• Elected to the student council two years in a row as secretary and activities social chair.
• Organized and participated in school's drive to raise $5,000 for people devastated by fire.
• Computer proficient in Microsoft Office Suite, Photoshop and various social media.
• Chosen as captain of cheerleading team that won the 2015 Cheerleading State Championship.
• Participated in school play, helped design stage and costumes for the cast.

References available upon request.

Notice that in the achievements section of the functional resume, the bullet points are short and to the point. This gives you the opportunity to expand on each of the highlighted points during the interview. For example, when speaking about the student council, you can elaborate on the responsibilities and duties of each position to the hiring manager. It's a good idea to make some notes regarding your achievements as a reference cheat sheet that you will have with you during the interview.

Just before or even during the interview, you can briefly glance at your notes as a reminder of what you want to convey to the hiring manager. Your notes should be in bullet form and easy to read. This is a good practice because you might feel nervous during the interview. A quick glance at your notes helps to refocus your mind and incorporates them into the conversation. Feeling nervous before or during an interview is normal. When feeling nervous, acknowledge it to yourself. Take a few deep breaths, which will help calm your nerves.

View every interview as an opportunity to sharpen your skills and make an effort to gain insight from each interaction. The information you provide to the hiring manager about yourself will determine if you are a good fit for the position. If you speak another language, make sure to include it on your resume.

In the chronological resume, your experience is highlighted just after the education portion. Notice that on both sample resumes, action verbs are used in the achievements and experience sections. These are the skills you have demonstrated through internships, part-time or summer jobs, coursework, leadership experience, volunteer or community service.

There are *three simple rules* to follow when creating your resume:

1. Proof read your resume. Have someone else proof read it too.
2. Focus on quantifiable accomplishments and be genuine. Honesty is the best policy!
3. Tailor your resume to the position. Find ways to include words or short phrases from the desired job description. These three rules cannot be emphasized enough!

There are *four skills* that every student has been developing in high school and that almost every employer is looking for:

1. dependable/responsible – studying for tests and meeting deadlines
2. quick learner – certain subjects or areas you excelled in
3. teamwork – working in groups

4. technology skills – most young adults have these skills

Following are several categories that contain a list of action verbs that can be incorporated into your resume. Do not limit yourself to this list only. You will notice that some of these action verbs are listed in more than one category. Action words can also be used to describe your job duties. Spend time reviewing your school accomplishments. They include the clubs you participated in and what role you played.

Communication	Clerical or Detail	Creative
arranged	approved	acted
collaborated	catalogued	created
convinced	classified	customized
developed	compiled	designed
directed	edited	established
drafted or edited	generated	founded
interpreted	implemented	illustrated
moderated	monitored	initiated
persuaded	operated	integrated
promoted	organized	introduced
publicized	prepared	invented
recruited	purchased	originated
translated	processed	performed
wrote	recorded	shaped

Management

analyzed
assigned
chaired
consolidated
coordinated
developed
directed
evaluated
improved
increased
organized
planned
prioritized
recommended

Helping

assessed
assisted
clarified
coached
counseled
demonstrated
educated
facilitated
tutored
familiarized
guided
motivated
referred
represented

Technical

assembled
calculated
computed
designed
devised
engineered
fabricated
maintained
operated
upgraded
programmed
remodeled
repaired
solved

Research

clarified
collected
critiqued
diagnosed
evaluated
examined
extracted
identified
inspected
interpreted
interviewed
investigated
organized
reviewed
summarized

Teaching

adapted
advised
communicated
developed
enabled
encouraged
explained
evaluated
facilitated
guided
instructed
informed
set goals
stimulated
trained

A Creative Exercise to Build Your Confidence

Many years ago, I learned an exercise that to this day I find very useful and worthwhile. When beginning any type of project, I use yellow post-it notes to quickly write down my ideas on separate pieces of paper. As each idea comes to mind, I write it on the post-it note and stick it on a wall or whiteboard. This process gets your creative juices flowing. Continue writing ideas and sticking them to the wall. Soon you will have a wall or whiteboard full of post-it notes.

As you begin to look at the notes, you'll find that some ideas belong together. Then you can begin to categorize the ideas and thoughts that belong together on one portion of the wall. The project starts to take shape and comes into focus. This is a constructive exercise that builds confidence. You will find that many ideas come out of the process. This exercise can be done on your own or in collaboration with others. When done as a group effort, it is very effective to get the ball rolling. You can complete this exercise in one day or over several days depending on the magnitude of your goal.

I recommend using this technique to create your resume. The four skills listed earlier that every employer is looking for can be your starting point. For example, technology skills - write on separate post it notes all the software and technology skills you have acquired such as MS Word, MS Excel and Power Point – you get the idea. Then continue the process for each category listed. This exercise builds confidence in your skills and abilities and demonstrates how creative you are.

References

References are people who know you, know your character and who would be willing to provide a prospective employer a good recommendation. Do you have a list of references? Your list of references can be one, two or even more individuals who have known you for a period of time (not family members). If you developed a positive relationship with a high school teacher or counselor, this could lead to a wonderful reference. Additionally, if you worked during high school, even if the job was part-time, your supervisor could be another excellent reference. Also, if you did any volunteer work during high school, the person who oversaw your volunteer work could be a personal reference. Did you tutor any students? If your tutoring made a difference, perhaps his/her parent might be willing to provide a personal recommendation.

Make sure your references know that you will be using them as a reference. First, ask for their permission and ensure that they will provide a positive recommendation. It is also a good idea to know which contact method they prefer: work phone, cell number or email. Let your references know about the position you are applying for. It will provide them a greater understanding of the job you are applying for. Remember, this person is supporting your efforts to find a job and will be happy to assist you.

Once you get the job, send a thank you note to your references and let them know you got the job. Also, another thank you note must be sent to the interviewer after the interview has taken place. If you interviewed with more than one person, then each person gets a thank you note. Whether it is a personal hand-written note, a text or an email, it will show them your appreciation and gratitude. Handwritten thank you notes are so rare today that if you choose to send one, it will certainly distinguish you. I highly suggest a hand-written note. Thank you notes can be simple and to the point. Whatever medium you choose to send a thank you note, it is a sure and definite way to make a positive impression.

Also remember that "thank you" notes are especially necessary for family and friends when they go out of their way to provide gifts for special occasions such as birthdays, Christmas or any other noteworthy events.

Here are two examples:

Dear Mr./Ms.,

Thank you for your time yesterday. I enjoyed meeting you and look forward to the next step in the process.

Sincerely,
Your Name

Dear Mr./Ms.,

Just a quick note to thank you for the time you've invested with me today.

Sincerely,
Your Name

This is exactly how simple, direct and to the point a thank you note should be. It takes less than a minute, and it just might be how you distinguish yourself from other candidates.

"References Available upon Request" is usually listed at the bottom of the page. Listing this phrase is a personal choice, as today's hiring managers assume you have references. When asked for references, having a prepared list available would demonstrate your assertive preparation skills and end the interview on a positive note.

Following is an example of the necessary elements needed in your reference list and should be on a separate piece of paper.

References for Mark Smith
1234 Homewood Drive, Any Town, USA 12345
Tel. (123) 456-7890
your.name@gmail.com

Mr. John Adams
Guidance Counselor
Anytown Senior High School
123-456-7890
John.adams@anytownhighschool.com

Mrs. Isabel Gutierrez
Title:
Company Name:
Phone:
Email:

Chapter 4

How to Research a Company

Sometimes you have to become a sleuth! On one job search, I came across an employment ad that did not have a company name. They requested candidates to fax their resumes to a listed phone number. Fax is an old technology that was used to transmit documents quickly. How do you research a company without knowing the name? Reading the employment ad several times provided some clues where it mentioned that this was a "newly created position" for a Fortune 500 company requiring Spanish speaking skills and travel. The candidate also had to be people-oriented, which in today's terminology equals social skills. After some consideration, I decided to respond. My first thought was how to distinguish myself "above" all others. The one area that came to mind was my Spanish speaking and writing abilities. So, I submitted the cover letter in both languages, and in addition, I highlighted my people-oriented skills as they related to other positions I had previously held. Then, I provided quick examples of how I solved people problems, submitted my resume and waited.

Sometimes in life, we must do some investigative work to find the information we require. One day a report regarding the aviation industry caught my eye. Since I like to stay on top of current business news (up to date information is of the utmost importance), in that moment a light bulb went on for me. It was about the same Fortune 500 company mentioned above that was acquiring the Latin American routes of a now bankrupt airline. I looked at the fax number, dialed similar numbers, and to my amazement, I was able to speak with someone and find out which company they represented. So, I had figured out what major airline had my resume. Given all this new information, now my mission was to conduct targeted research and prepare myself as well as I could. There was no doubt in my mind that I would land an interview, and then the call came a few weeks later. After several rounds of interviews with various C-level executives, I was offered the prized position.

When seeking employment, there were some ads that initially interested me; however, after further consideration I felt differently. So, it is truly important to give yourself time to reflect on the ad and the open position. Some people see an ad, find their resume, quickly put together a cover letter and send it off. Every time I responded to an opening, I tailored my resume for the specific position. While some people might think it involves rewriting the entire resume, it does not.

My strategy is to save a resume copy in a new folder under the name of the prospective company and the same for the cover letter. This strategy enabled me to go back and tweak the language to match my skills and abilities to what companies were seeking in a candidate. So, when I was called for an interview, I just had to look in the resume folder for the company name and print a few copies. It is an easy system to incorporate into your job search action. Finally, always remember to periodically review this resume folder and delete the files that are no longer active.

Why do you need to research the company? There are two main reasons for conducting your research. The research will help you determine if the company is *where you would like to work and to prepare you for the interview*. Additionally, in this chapter, I will provide valuable insight and tips for answering interview questions. The research will also depend on the size of the company and their presence in the marketplace. The obvious beginning point is the company website. Listed below are some of the information points that can be very useful in determining if it's the right company for you.

- the corporate culture and working conditions
- the mission of the company
- industry trends
- major competitors
- number of employees

As you continue to research the company, it's a good idea to make copious notes. The entire research process should be one that helps you identify if this is the right work environment for you. Sometimes a candidate's only consideration is to present themselves as a good fit for the company. They might feel pressured to find employment quickly. Equally as important would be to determine if an employer or organization is a good match for *you.* It serves no purpose to be hired then three months later, you find it is not a good match, and you are not happy.

Knowing where to conduct your research is the first step in preparing for the interview. The most obvious starting point is the internet. If you don't have a computer, they are available at most libraries. Also, the library has free news articles from the local newspapers. Look for trade publications which can provide excellent information, and the library staff is most certain to assist in your efforts. Trade publications are magazines that focus specifically on their industries and can provide excellent insight and information to assist in your research. Your local chamber of commerce website will have information on the industry leaders in your community that are expanding, growing and looking for new enthusiastic employees. The more information you acquire, the better prepared and confident you will be during the interview.

Hiring managers will ask questions during the interview process to determine if you understand their organization. There are different types of questions you should be prepared to answer. So please take a notepad, a pen and two or three copies of your resume to every interview. You might be thinking they already have my resume, and yes, I agree with you. However, it is a common practice to ask for your resume at the interview. If you are interviewing with the Human Resources representative, they might refer you to meet with someone else. So, always have at least three copies with you for an interview. The same goes for the list of references. It is best to be over prepared, and don't forget to have your list of questions to ask the interviewer as well.

Here are a few examples of the types of questions you will likely be asked.

General questions about the company and why you believe you are a good fit for them. This is where all the research you previously conducted will ensure you answer with confidence. From the company's website, you will gain insight into their mission statement, corporate culture and career opportunities. Knowing what kind of employees the company looks to hire conveys to the hiring manager that you have done your research. Make sure to investigate every aspect of a company's website to gain as much relevant information for your application.

Behavioral questions require you to provide actual examples of skills and experiences that relate directly to the available position. The interviewer might ask you to tell of a time when you had to complete a project or work together with others under a very tight deadline. They are looking for the kinds of behaviors you might exhibit in order to complete the task in the specific timeframe and how well you work with others.

These behavioral questions could start with:

- Tell me about a time when you encountered a challenging situation and how you handled it.
- Describe how you set goals for yourself.
- Tell me about how you work on a team.
- Have you ever made a mistake? (Who has not?) Tell me how you handled it.

The key to answering these questions is to be clear, concise and truthful. Present the experiences by using real examples and highlighting the situations where you were successful. Here you will find more examples: https://www.thebalance.com/behavioral-job-interview-questions-2059620

Thinking of these types of questions and your responses in advance will increase and build your confidence level. I recommend creating a list of behavioral questions as an exercise to strengthen your proficiency. Practice answering behavioral questions out loud on your own and build your confidence. Practice the same scenario with a trusted family member or friend and ask them for feedback. A popular, practice strategy called "STAR Technique" is explained in the following paragraph.

S T A R Technique
S = Situation   T = Task   A = Action   R = Results

Describe the *situation* where you performed the job or faced a challenge (it can be a work experience, volunteer position or school scenario). Next, describe the *task,* which was your responsibility in the situation. Then, specifically describe the *action* showing how you completed the task or resolved the challenge. Finally, explain the *results* or the outcomes generated by the action taken. The key to the STAR technique is to describe the situation by being specific and to the point. It is important to remember to highlight your contributions when answering behavioral questions.

Situational questions ask you to consider possible situations in the workplace. They are used to elicit the candidate's skills for the specific job. Situational questions ask you to describe a particular case. If you list "great people skills" on your resume, you might be asked how you would handle a difficult customer. Describe a time you had to handle a difficult co-worker or manager. Describe a situation where you had to convince someone to change their point of view about something. Describe a time you had to take the initiative. Describe a time when you received constructive criticism. These situational questions are searching to find your people skills, organizational skills, how you set priorities, communication skills and problem-solving abilities.

Like behavioral questions, you can use prior experiences to answer these types of questions. As well as you can, use examples that are closely related to the job description of the position you are interviewing for.

Tell me about yourself needs to be answered in a straightforward manner about your education and work history *as it relates to the position.* During the interview, engaging in conversation that is not related to the position, defeats the interviewer's purpose. You may be asked to describe your strengths and weaknesses. Select a trait and come up with a solution to either highlight the strength or overcome the weakness. It is always best to keep the job description in mind and avoid weaknesses that would make you unfit for the job. Here is an example: "Sometimes I am very critical of myself when I make mistakes; however, I have learned that making mistakes is part of the learning process." At this point, the interviewer might ask you to provide an example. So be prepared!

Entry level candidate interview questions will typically focus on why you are interested in the position and why the company should hire you. This is an opportunity to review and highlight your skills and how they match up to the job description. Speak in terms of what contributions you see yourself making and how the company will benefit by hiring you for this position. The hiring manager might also ask where you see yourself in five to ten years. The reason behind this kind of questioning is to determine if you have established mid-range and long-range goals for yourself. Setting goals is essential to your success. If you have not already done so, set some goals for yourself. Setting goals is not as complicated as it may seem. The key to setting goals is to write them down. The power of the written word will surprise you. Set some short-term goals – one to two years and put them in an envelope in a safe place in your home. After a year has passed, look for the envelope, and you just might surprise yourself. The benefit of this exercise is that when you are asked about your goals in life, you will be prepared with answers.

Your questions for the hiring manager are just as important in the process. It demonstrates your interest in the company and the position. Many candidates take a passive role in the interview when it comes to *asking* questions. They competently answer the questions that are put to them and are never able to take the initiative by asking intelligent questions that steer the interview in a helpful direction. If you are a proactive candidate who asks questions, then you will be seen as a more dynamic and interested candidate. It can significantly increase your chances of being offered the job.

Following are a few examples of questions, and they are in no particular order.

What would be my day-to-day responsibilities? This is an example of your communication skills at work. It is essential that you clearly understand what is expected of you and the tasks at hand. It is easy to make assumptions and get the wrong impressions of what the position requires. So, it is of the utmost importance that it be made clear to you, and if something is unclear have a follow-up question. You are asking instead of assuming.

What are the opportunities for training and career advancement? There are two reasons to ask this question. It helps you to understand where this position might lead within the company, and it also indicates you are ambitious and thinking of the future.

What are the criteria you are looking for in the successful candidate for this position? The job description probably listed what they are looking for in a candidate; however, it is extremely useful to hear the criteria directly from the interviewer. When the interviewer mentions something that resonates with you (one of your skills), it's your opportunity to reiterate why you are a good candidate for this position.

How do you feel I measure up to the requirements for this position? This question is a good one following the previous question and may seem a bit bold. It is a fair question to ask and provides the interviewer an opportunity to give you honest feedback. Receive the input, evaluate it and use it to develop your skill set. Every face to face meeting you have is an opportunity to polish your interview abilities and skills.

When did you join? To ask the interviewer this question is entirely your choice. After the interviewer has asked lots of questions about you, it may be a good time to shift and ask something about them. People love to talk about themselves, and if you can get them to share some of their experiences in the company, it might provide valuable information for you.

Is this a newly created position? How long has the position been vacant? If it is a newly created position, you have the opportunity to be creative and make the position yours. During my career, there were several "new positions," which was a bit scary for me, since I did not know what to expect. What resulted was the opportunity for me to create several dream jobs. If the position was vacated, try to learn why or how long the previous person was there and how quickly they are looking for a replacement. The answers to these questions can provide clues to the position.

Are there any other questions I can answer for you? If the interviewer says no, then this is your opportunity to summarize what you have learned about the position and sell them on why you are a good fit for the job. You must be proactive and remind them why you are the right candidate for the position.

Answer all questions with integrity and honesty. Always keep in mind the job description when answering questions during the interview. Bring a notepad to write down important facts. Make sure you are making eye contact during the interview, listening actively and contributing to the conversation. When candidates take notes during the interview, it sends a very positive message that they are interested. Before you walk into the company, make sure to put your phone on "airplane/silent" mode. If you use the "vibrate" mode, it can be an unwanted distraction during the meeting. Better yet, leave the phone in your car. While you may disagree, the temptation to check your phone during the interview is no longer there. Checking your phone during an interview sends a message that your phone is more important than the interview.

From the moment you step onto the company property, you must assume everyone is assessing you. You may not realize it, but your demeanor and actions speak volumes. Numerous times I have been told the candidate did not get the job due to the perception that they seemed more interested in their phones than in the interview. I know of a case where a candidate, waiting for his interview appointment in the lobby of a company, was asked by an employee walking by if he needed assistance. With his eyes cast down on his phone, the candidate waved no with his hand dismissing the kind gesture of the employee. Later, I learned he did not get the job because of that action. In that instance, there were two candidates up for the newly created position. I was the other candidate who did get the job.

A friendly smile, a poised presence and staying off social media while you are waiting to be called in for the interview will send a very positive message. If you think no one is looking, think again. Today, cameras are everywhere, and someone is always watching.

Chapter 5

What Defines a Valuable Employee?

Valuable is defined as something that has great monetary worth. A valuable employee is recognized for their efforts and valued for their contributions to the company or organization. As a paid employee, one receives monetary compensation. However, there are additional characteristic attributes that identify a valuable employee.

When I worked at my first job in the bakery, I acknowledged everyone as they walked in the door. Each time the door opened, a bell sound triggered, so I knew when a customer walked in. Then, I would make eye contact, smile and say, "Hello, I will be right with you." Many were repeat customers, and over time I learned their names. Frequently, I was the only person working behind the counter and got slammed with customers. Since the bakery was not a large space, acknowledging customers with a smile as they walked in the door simply made sense to me. It was a habit I created early on in my life.

So, one day out of the blue, the bakery owner came over and thanked me for doing a great job. As the conversation continued, he specifically mentioned how he loved that I referred to our customers by their names. I will never forget how he said, "Carmen, you are a valuable employee here!" Keep in mind, when you first set out to remember people's names, it will take some effort on your part. With practice, it becomes easier, and before you know it, you will have created a great habit for life.

The name given to us at birth is the sweetest name on earth. So, if you have the opportunity to address people by their first name, make that choice. It is still a habit that I continue to use each day in my life. Wherever I go, if someone is wearing a name tag, I consider it an invitation to use their name in our conversation. Keep in mind that it is important to speak to your superiors with the utmost respect by always addressing these individuals with their respective titles such as Mr., Ms., Mrs., Sir, etc.

What are the traits and characteristics of a valuable employee? How do you become a valuable employee?

Every business organization, large or small, functions in its own specific and unique way. Employment opportunities can vary immensely by geographic location and industry. Potential employees frequently need to solve problems and be adaptable to changes. There are some top characteristics and traits that businesses, in general, seem to value in their employees.

Have you ever heard of **hard skills**? Hard skills as defined by investopia.com are specific teachable abilities that can be defined and measured, such as typing, writing, math, reading and the ability to use software programs such as publisher or PowerPoint. Also, playing an instrument is an example of a hard skill. Hard skills are specific abilities that can be defined and measured.

Have you ever heard of **soft skills**? Soft skills are more difficult to quantify and measure and are highly valued everywhere by employers. Soft skills encompass a wide range of capabilities that include social graces, communication abilities, language skills, personal habits, cognitive or emotional empathy, time management, teamwork and leadership traits. Soft skills are more related to personality than ability. Today, many employers, depending on their needs, are looking for candidates who offer a combination of hard and soft skills.

Outlined below are some traits and characteristics that will no doubt make you a valuable employee.

Having a strong work ethic is tremendously valued by employers. An employee with a strong, disciplined, moral work ethic has a sense of responsibility, is concerned about the quality of their work and is someone who sets high goals. One who is willing to do more than is required and demonstrates the ability to be stretched beyond their comfort zone shows a willingness to be flexible and adapt to the situation.

Let's say you have worked on a project that is due on Monday morning. Everything you were tasked to do was completed on Friday. Over the weekend, you thought of an additional element that could add value to the project. Instead of coming in at 9am on Monday morning, you choose to arrive at 7am to update your work. By coming in extra early, you've demonstrated a strong work ethic going above and beyond what was assigned to you.

Dependability and *reliability* go hand in hand, and employers treasure these attributes in their employees. Once you are part of a team, the company needs your commitment to follow through on your responsibilities. Calling in sick because you simply don't "feel well" does not cut it. Arriving to work on time, returning phone calls in a timely manner, taking the appropriate lunchtime, performing tasks on time and working past quitting time will let your employer know you are dependable and reliable. Strive to achieve a consistent level of quality and excellence. Finally, let's not forget simple commitments.

Active listening and *being responsive* can have an infinitely positive impact on your career. Active listening is all about being present and clearly understanding the information required to execute your job. You might not realize that active listening is a form of communication. When a supervisor sees you are patiently listening to them without interruption, they will be assured you are taking them and your duties seriously. It also shows respect to those attempting to guide you. Reflecting on the information and repeating back what you've heard will save you time and heartache. Repeating back information is not necessary for every situation. Nevertheless, it is a good habit since all of us listen through different filters. Today, it is not very common to find an individual who waits and listens before acting.

Being responsive is really very simple and easy. When someone addresses you, kindly respond by letting them know you've heard them. When your response is animated and enthusiastic, you are engaged in effective communication, and people take notice. This is a common courtesy and will distinguish you from others who routinely say nothing but stare blankly into space. Responding to people is just another way of showing them they matter.

Taking responsibility is another essential quality employers find valuable. In taking ownership of the behavior and accepting the consequences of that behavior, you will develop self-respect and even the respect of others. While taking responsibility, you might consider looking for solutions rather than being hard on yourself. From making mistakes, I've learned the results produced were not the results I wanted to achieve. So, I tried again to produce a different result. Most people do not want to admit their mistakes since they believe it makes them look weak. Admitting your mistakes is viewed more as a sign of maturity rather than as a weakness.

Does having a *positive attitude* sound too obvious as a character trait hiring managers are looking for today? Positivity can lead to a more productive workplace environment hence employers are looking for a positive attitude in their candidates. When a candidate has the ability to acknowledge mistakes and moves forward with a positive attitude, they can earn a favorable reputation within the company. Who doesn't like to be around an enthusiastic and upbeat person? Positive, cheerful attitudes are contagious!

A *team-oriented* person is valuable to employers since a company is not one individual. There is no letter "I" in the word team. The ability to collaborate with others is critical, as everyone brings a different skill set to the workplace. You may learn from others, and others will learn from you. Working in a team environment requires patience and respect for others, and it builds trust. Collaborating in a team environment provides the opportunity for you to practice giving credit to others. In a team environment, whenever you are complimented for a job well done, always share the spotlight with those who've helped you succeed. When you are acknowledged, it's an opportunity to say thank you to all the team members, and it will improve and strengthen morale among the team. It will also build trust, as they will be confident you'll look out and speak up for them, especially when no one else will.

Working effectively with little direction is the definition of a *self-motivated* and *confident* employee. Hiring managers are keenly aware that candidates with initiative are very valuable to their organization if they can get the work done with little to no encouragement. When you are confident in your abilities, it will drive your motivation to excel in your work. Self-motivated employees are consistent performers, problem solvers, results-oriented, adaptable to change, flexible and they honor deadlines. A self-motivated employee with initiative is an asset to a company and can easily work their way up the career ladder. If you see something that is out of place, take the initiative and put it back in its place. When working at a company that has a kitchen and the coffee pot is empty, take the initiative and make a new pot of coffee. The more you take the initiative, the more people will notice.

Employers place a high value on *effective communicators*. These individuals understand the benefits of clarity and the importance of good communication skills. It sounds so simple, yet all too often we say one thing and the other person hears something else. You can create value by instigating consistent and complete communication that keeps everyone informed. If something is not clear to you, ask for clarification. In a team environment, there may be others who are also unclear on how to proceed with an assignment. What if you are the only one who asks for clarification? *Think about that for a moment.* Since you were the only one with the courage to speak up, you may be thought of as the hero.

If you are *a problem solver,* you are a tremendous asset to the company. Solving problems are at the center of what many people do at work today. Problem-solving skills are highly desirable since problem solvers can identify the issues at hand from everyone's perspective. Your oral and written communications skills will play an important part in being clear about and understanding the circumstances. Your perception of the problem may be different from what others on your team may experience. Coming up with possible solutions, collaborating with others and evaluating the options by asking what the pluses and minuses are, are all strategies that could lead to a positive resolution.

These are just a few examples of how you can become a valuable company employee. Once employed, you may be required to attend company training sessions that will increase both your hard and soft skills.

How to Distinguish Yourself from Others

What matters most in the end are the *small details.* When you consistently set a high standard for yourself, others will take notice. Some of these relevant and important life skills are simple to implement. Others require your razor-sharp focus and continued practice in order to perfect. There are also some personal qualities that people who distinguish themselves have incorporated into their lives. Using these life skills and personal qualities will enable you to make the best of everyday life. By putting them into action, you will begin the process of distinguishing yourself from others.

1. *Listen to your self-talk.* Notice the internal conversation you are having with yourself. If you notice negative self-talk, immediately say *stop* and think of the why. Saying stop out loud has power. If you made a mistake, correct it and tell yourself you will do better next time. Recognize that your internal conversations affect how you view yourself and how you react to others. Life is a journey and being hard on yourself simply makes the journey more difficult. *Lighten up!*

2. *Your appearance matters.* Whether you think so or not, a first impression is largely based on your overall look that includes what you wear and how you style

your hair. So, if you don't believe me, how many times have you judged someone by their appearance? Choosing the appropriate attire for the specific occasion is important. A polished look is one way of distinguishing yourself from others. A polished look for men is an ironed shirt that is tucked into your pants with a belt around the waist and clean shoes. For ladies, a length appropriate skirt, dress or suit with minimal jewelry, styled hair and manicured nails. Taking the time to ensure your shoes are clean and polished is just one small detail that matters.

3. *A firm handshake.* There is nothing worse when shaking someone's hand that feels like a dead fish. It comes across as weak and even uninterested. Of course, you don't want to crush their bones either! A handshake is your opportunity to express your confidence, and it speaks louder than words. Notice how someone shakes your hand; it tells you a lot about them – be observant.

4. *Eye contact is a form of non-verbal communication.* This is not as simple as it sounds. When speaking with one person, it is acceptable to look away occasionally to gather your thoughts. When you are listening to someone, it is important to maintain eye contact. It is a sign of respect and demonstrates you are taking a genuine interest in what they have to

say. When you find yourself in a group setting, place your full attention on the person who is speaking. If you are the speaker in a group setting, pause and share your eye contact equally with each individual.

5. *Being on time shows respect.* When you get into the habit of being on time all the time, you are less stressed. You send a strong message that indicates you honor your commitment, can be trusted and are dependable and reliable.

6. *Remembering names.* Many people believe they don't have the skill to remember names. They simply don't take the time and energy to concentrate and repeat the name in their minds in order to remember. This is another small detail that matters. Begin to practice daily and build instant rapport with the new people you meet. Start by paying attention when you are introduced to someone. If you didn't catch their name, don't be shy to ask, "What is your name?" Get into the habit by immediately repeating their name saying, "Nice to meet you, Jane." During the conversation, repeat their name several times in your head and out loud. By saying it out loud, it will assist you to remember their name. If you are given a business card, look at it and repeat their name. If you simply put the card away without looking at their name, you are missing

an opportunity to acknowledge the sweetest name on earth to them: their name.

7. *Never forget the magic words "Please" and "Thank You."* We were all taught to say please and thank you when growing up. Throughout life, you will discover we all rely on assistance from others, both professionally and personally. When you use the word "please" with a smile and a genuine tone, people are more willing to go out of their way to help you. The words "thank you" are a form of acknowledgment that says, "I appreciate what you do for me." You become well-respected when you thank people for their time, for their efforts and for their assistance. If someone pays you a compliment, don't shrug it off as if it were nothing. It could convey a lack of self-respect and might be interpreted that their appreciation for you is meaningless. A simple, heartfelt thank you is an opportunity for them to recognize gratitude during your encounter.

Make an effort to incorporate these small details into your life, and before you know it, they will become good habits.

1. Listening to your self-talk – keep it positive.
2. Choosing appropriate attire for the occasion – your appearance matters.

3. Having a firm handshake – conveys confidence.
4. Making eye contact is a form of non-verbal communication – it expresses genuine interest.
5. Being on time shows respect – sends a strong message that you honor your commitment.
6. Remembering names – builds instant rapport with the people you meet.
7. Saying please and thank you – recognizes the other person and expresses gratitude for their actions.

Seek out personal and professional growth training and development opportunities that will enhance your overall value as an individual. The greatest investment you make is in yourself.

Chapter 6

Essential Everyday Life Skills

In addition to what and how much you have learned in school, "important life skills" are critical for success no matter what stage of life you are in. It is up to you to make a commitment to take charge of your life. Some of these skills are simple to incorporate. Others take time, determination, practice and perseverance. The clarity of communication and the quality of connection with others will positively impact relationships throughout your lifetime. Continually developing these skills is an essential component of professional success. Communicating effectively is the most important life skill you'll need.

Communication Skills

Everything you do in life is about communicating with others. Your communication skills will have an impact on all the personal, professional and social relationships during your lifetime. Communication is about being able to clearly convey information, effectively from one place to another. Some of us find it easy to communicate our thoughts, feelings and emotions, while others find it difficult. Information is provided verbally from a distance as over the phone or in a video, and in person face-to-face. We also communicate through our body language and via the written word.

Now let's start with verbal communication. Verbal communication serves as a vehicle for expressing desires, ideas and concepts. A variety of challenges may result when using verbal communication to express oneself. Misunderstandings can arise because of a poor choice of words. In addition, when you add the cultural component, the message itself can be confusing. You may not realize there are cultural differences in our country. What you say and how you say it matters.

Sometimes our body language speaks louder than our words. Have you ever been on a flight where suddenly, the airplane hits a patch of turbulence? In this situation, who's the first person you might look for? If you are like most people, you may look for reassurance from a flight attendant. Part of the rigorous training I received in the flight attendant academy was to become aware of my body language and the impact it can have on the passengers at any time. On a clear, sunny day during a flight from San Juan, Puerto Rico to JFK Airport, New York we suddenly hit a patch of heavy turbulence while over the Caribbean waters.

To this day, I have a clear memory of how the passengers all looked to the crew for reassurance that all was well. Written exams, simulator exercises, equipment hands-on and shouted out commands are just a few of the subjects I had to learn and memorize to perfection. Interpersonal skills, peer interactions and personal grooming habits were scrutinized daily. Also, the instructors found unique ways to test our tolerance levels, all designed to reveal the most hidden personality traits. Flight attendant training is designed to weed out the weakest links and typically lasts anywhere from six to twelve weeks depending on the airline. For me, successfully graduating from the flight attendant academy was an unforgettable experience, since much of what I learned then is still with me today.

Using the following tips requires a concerted effort on your part to practice, practice and practice some more. Your success in developing your communication skills is directly related to your ability to understand and proficiently learn the concepts below.

Tip #1   **Think Before You Speak**

To increase your chances of communicating successfully, *think* before you speak. Pause to clarify your message in your mind and speak thoughtfully, respectfully considering the recipient's point of view. Most of us just speak from our perspective. If you can put yourself in the other person's shoes for a moment, you might say it differently. Choose your words carefully.

Tip #2   **The Manner of Your Speaking**

Are you speaking too fast? Fast talkers may come across as very smart; however, behind their backs, they are frequently criticized. Some people may interpret fast talking as a sign of nervousness and a lack of self-confidence. Fast talking can also make it appear you don't think people want to listen or what you have to say is not important. If you are a fast talker, learn to pause between phrases or at the end of sentences. Fast talkers do not take in enough air; therefore, towards the end of a sentence, their voices lack volume and clarity.

Pausing, speaking slowly or cautiously, will make you sound more confident and strong. It also allows you to think while you are talking. If you are a fast talker, begin to slow your speaking by reading out loud, pausing for commas and periods. At first, it might feel silly, since you are used to speaking a certain way. With practice, you will find your middle ground. Or, are you speaking too slowly? People who speak too slowly can be rudely interrupted by others who lack the patience to listen.

Your tone of voice matters and can readily show disappointment or satisfaction in a conversation. The energy of your voice is a huge component of a winning tone and attracts people's attention. The correct manner of speaking should result in a conversation that flows back and forth, much like watching a tennis match. I recommend you observe others in their manner of speaking and make your own observations and conclusions.

Tip #3   **Ask Questions**

Questions in their simplest form can be open-ended or closed-ended. Closed-ended questions are typically answered with a yes or no. They have their own language and typically start with the following verbs: are, was, did, will, won't, didn't, aren't, would and if. To the person answering the question, it can seem like an interrogation. Closed-ended questions do not allow you to expand your communication skills. Open-ended questions require a person to pause, think and reflect. When responding to open-ended questions, you express creativity, and it allows for lots of information to flow. This invites people to open up and shows them you are interested in what they have to say. Typically, open-ended questions begin with the words "how, what, why, tell me and describe." Open-ended questions are a great way to connect with people and to break the ice. Knowing what types of questions to ask in any environment develops your overall social skill set.

Tip #4   Non-Verbal Communication

Many of us are unaware of the non-verbal communication messages we send out daily. The facial expressions, tone of voice, gestures, body language and the way we present ourselves, are all considered non-verbal communications. All of us use our facial expressions to convey emotions without saying a word. Through our facial expressions, we convey universal emotions of fear, disgust, anger, sadness, surprise and happiness. Appropriate eye contact goes hand in hand with facial expressions. It communicates our interest in the conversation and becomes a means of keeping the conversation going. Looking at a door and glancing at our watch sends a message that we want to exit the conversation. With the use of technology, we can convey our emotions through emoticons in our text messages and emails.

Your posture such as sitting tall, shoulders back with head held high conveys a confident, self-assured individual and will likely gain the respect of others. Body language goes hand in hand with posture, and if you are unaware of your own, it can easily be misinterpreted by others. Stop and think about the non-verbal messages you are sending out to others. All of us use non-verbal communication skills daily. The more aware you are of your own non-verbal messaging, the sooner you can make adjustments.

Tip #5   **Become a Good Listener**

A skilled communicator listens more than he speaks. When you provide others the opportunity to be heard and understood, they will walk away feeling empowered. When you become a good listener, you are helping others by meeting their needs, understanding their concerns and adding value to their world. People don't really care how much you know. They want to know that you really care. Becoming a good listener shows how much you care.

Tip # 6   Written Communication

Be thoughtful in your written communications, especially in emails. If you stop and think about emails, they are written words that are electronically sent, and we give meaning to those words. If you receive an email that makes you feel upset, wronged or mad, it's probably best to wait. If you choose to respond right away, it will more than likely be an emotional response. If possible, consider walking away, cooling off and maybe addressing the issue in person.

Grammar, punctuation and spelling matter. Writing is another form of communication that you need in order to respond appropriately to emails, convey your ideas and solve problems. Spelling shortcuts used in texting today are not appropriate in the workplace. You must clearly understand the importance of your writing skills; there's always room for improvement.

An example of your writing skills is reflected on your resume. Is the language simple and to the point? How will you address a letter of complaint to a landlord? A simple way to improve your writing skills is by just writing. Choose a subject that interests you and get started. Then find someone you trust, perhaps an older mentor type person and share your writings with them. Let them know you are looking to improve your writing skills and would like some constructive feedback. There are many people with a wealth of knowledge and information that are willing to help. It is up to you to make it happen.

Time Management

Think of your time as money! Spend it wisely. Life will be less stressful when you learn to manage your time. The sooner you train yourself to manage time effectively, the more time you will have to do other things. There will be fewer surprises, fewer deadlines and less rushing from task to task or place to place. You will experience less friction and problems such as forgotten appointments or missed deadlines. For many, time management means trying to find a way to be as productive as possible 24 hours a day, when in reality it's not!

Either you control the day, or the day controls you!

Time management was not something my parents taught me growing up. I did not clearly understand how critical it was until I lived on my own. Working in a variety of industries and positions, I learned the importance of managing my time, including time for myself. Spending a total of eight years in the aviation industry, I learned how others depended on my punctuality. Being a flight attendant for four years taught me firsthand how to be "on time all the time." While living in NYC, one of the most coveted trip assignments in the winter season was Acapulco, Mexico.

The long layover in the sun was always fun, and on one such trip, I met Sylvester Stallone who was filming Rambo at the time. Being the designated Spanish speaker, I loved this trip assignment. One morning, I arrived 10 minutes late and had already been replaced. I begged the crew schedulers to reassign me, and they simply said, "You missed your check-in time." After that incident, I never missed a check-in time again. Later, I learned that working in the corporate world was different.

There, I had the freedom to create my own schedule. At times, this was also challenging due to hard deadlines and the need to be on time for scheduled department meetings among other things. In my various positions, there were many weekdays that I worked late into the evening hours to ensure I was fulfilling my duties. There were many Saturdays as well, spent working in the office instead of being out having fun with friends. What I was unaware of at the time, was that I did not know how to manage my time effectively. Ultimately, the stress from the endless work schedules and a lack of time management skills landed me in the hospital on a few occasions. These were difficult lessons to learn that taught me the importance of managing my time more efficiently. Today, there are so many ways we waste time without realizing it.

When you manage your time, you avoid creating problems by properly planning ahead. Track your time for at least one week, and you will see whether you are devoting enough time to the projects and people most meaningful to you. Prioritize your time by tackling tasks that demand the most concentration and creativity during the times you feel most focused. Plan a schedule and stick to it. Scheduling is the key. Block out a window of time on a specific date to tackle a specific job. Prevent the interruptions by silencing your phone and closing the door if necessary. Focus intently for about 45-50 minutes, stop and take a short break to refresh your mind; then you will feel invigorated to continue.

A common misconception of time management is that it takes extra effort when in fact, it's quite the contrary, *it makes your life easier.* What it does take is discipline. One of its greatest benefits is that your time management reputation will follow you. Whether at work, in school or in life, you will be known as a reliable individual. Following is a list of suggestions to get you started. They all apply to your home, school and/or work life.

1. *Make a to-do list every day.* Begin by creating separate to-do lists for home and work and prioritize them.

Put the most important or difficult tasks on top, even if they are things you dread. These are the actions that require your undivided attention and focus. As you work your way down the list, include tasks you look forward to doing as an incentive to get the difficult things done first. When on that day, you complete everything on your list, you are done. Congratulations! If there is anything leftover on your daily to-do list, roll it into tomorrow's list.

Once you get into the habit of making lists and writing them down, you won't have to remember everything. It will become a good habit to help organize your life. There are many apps available today exactly for this purpose. For your home to-do list, include things like laundry, buy groceries and clean bedroom or bathroom. Be specific about the tasks on your to-do list. The more specific you are, the more likely you are to complete the task. For example: "hang picture vs. hang dining room picture." If you have several pictures to hang, then you might say I don't know where to start. If your list says, "hang dining room picture," once it's completed, you have a measurable result. The to-do lists are all about measuring your own results. When you see your list getting smaller, you will feel empowered with a great sense of accomplishment.

If, during the work week, you think of additional home tasks, simply add them to your list. Once the weekend rolls around, you'll have a game plan ready to go. Simple and easy. If you do not complete the home to-do list this weekend, then you've already created one for next weekend. The same concept applies to your work life. Early on Friday afternoons, it's a good idea to get into the habit of creating a work to-do list for the upcoming week. So, when you come in on Monday, you already have a game plan for the week.

2. *Learn how to say no.* Perhaps growing up or during your high school days, all the people around you (parents, family, friends, academic counselors, etc.) probably encouraged you to do more or to get involved in clubs. When you are asked to do something or get involved in a community event, out of kindness your *automatic response might be yes.* Learning to say no is a way of managing your time. You and only you can pick and choose where and how you would like to spend your time. Be aware the next time you are invited to "do something" and how quickly you might say yes. Learn to prioritize when and where to invest your time. Listen to your automatic responses. We all have them. Now, I'm not saying that you should never volunteer your

time and efforts to help others. It is simply meant to make you aware of how you spend your time and to understand that every single one of us needs down time to recharge our batteries. I am not condoning selfishness all the time, but you do need chilling time alone to replenish your energy levels.

3. *Find your most productive time.* Face it, some of us are morning people, and some of us are night owls. Understanding when you are most productive will help you be more efficient.

4. *Create dedicated time periods for yourself.* Set up a time devoted only to the specific task you want to complete. This goes hand in hand with finding your most productive time. Consider yourself a student of life, no matter what your age. Whenever you are studying, make it an uninterrupted and focused learning time slot. During this period, turn off your phone and respond to calls and texts only after your work is finished. When in a work environment, you can use the same approach. Determine if an immediate response is needed otherwise respond to emails once in the morning and once in the afternoon.

5. *Don't get sidetracked.* There are distractions all around us, and it is so easy to get sidetracked. For most people, technology is the number one

distraction that wastes time. If you find yourself distracted and wasting time, as we all do, stop and go back to your to-do list. If you are unsure on how to proceed or move forward with a task, go to your manager or supervisor and ask for assistance. If this is the case in a learning environment, get clarity from the instructor.

6. *Budget your time.* By creating "activity schedules," you will learn how to best manage your time. This will determine how much free time you have before you make additional commitments. To get started, I would suggest printing a free monthly calendar off the internet. Following is a free PDF blank calendar link, which you can fill in and print. This will allow you to better understand how to budget your time. http://www.cegeon.com/plain_printable_calendar. pdf

Printing a hard copy and making your notes, helps to see the entire month and where you are spending your time. At the end of the month, you can go back and review your accomplishments. If there was anything left undone, add it to next month's calendar. As you become more efficient at budgeting your time, you may choose an alternative method of scheduling. Keep in mind that it takes approximately three weeks to form new habits, and once you begin this process, it will become more natural.

7. *Prior planning prevents poor performance.* This can prove to be true in every area of your life. Contrary to what you might think, prior planning can take just a few minutes and can predict your future. The money I saved from working at the bakery made it possible to purchase my first car. At the time, I was unaware of the additional expenses and responsibilities that come with the purchase of a car, stuff like insurance, oil changes, tires and general maintenance.

So, let's look at buying a car. Determine the kind of vehicle you would like to buy: new or used, make, model and year, maintenance costs and gas consumption. Car insurance is another factor in the planning process, as some cars cost more to insure than others. Contact an insurance agent; provide them with the details of your intended purchase, and they will be able to quote the insurance rates for your age and location. By making a list of these considerations and how much they will cost each month, you'll have created a plan to purchase a car. If you find that what you want at this time is not aligned with your financial ability, you can choose a less expensive car or wait and save more money.

Another example of prior planning is the kind of apartment or home you would like to live in. Consider living on your own vs. living with a roommate. For either option, you will need to sign a lease. If you sign a lease on your own, it means you are solely responsible for the rent each month, but you are also free to live your own lifestyle. If the landlord allows for a joint lease, then both tenants are responsible. You might want to consider how living with one or more roommates will look like for you. Not everyone has the same level of tidiness or organization.

So, you might want to make a list of what is important to you. Some considerations include splitting groceries, utility bills, cooking, cleaning duties, and using, sharing or borrowing each other's belongings. Draw up a "Roommate Agreement" where all the ground rules are known in advance. All roommate situations are different and require respect, consideration, compromise and communication from all parties. These are just a few instances of how prior planning will save a lot of frustration and headaches down the road. When you invest some time and effort in planning for important things in your life, it will make a tremendous difference in the outcome.

8. *Make time for yourself!* It is easy to forget to make time for ourselves even if that means doing nothing or sleeping 12 hours a day. Getting the appropriate amount of sleep is vitally important, as it will re-energize you to be more productive.

In case you are wondering, I am not suggesting you plan for every single detail in your life. What I am suggesting is that you learn to plan for the important things and events in your life. The more you prepare and plan for your life, the easier and more stress-free your life will be!

"Chance always favors the prepared mind!"
Louis Pasteur

Money Management

Just like time management, if you are to be financially successful, learning how to manage your money is a vital and critical life skill. During my life, I met many people who expressed a desire to be financially successful but did not know how to go about it. It's possible to achieve your financial goals by successfully managing your money. Once you have learned time and money management skills, you'll find that you are living a more stress-free lifestyle.

Your financial success depends on your relationship to money. Many people do not realize that they have, or they lack a healthy relationship with money. Ask yourself the following questions:

What is my relationship with money? Am I controlling my bills or are my bills controlling me?

Having no consistent money strategies, no planning for the future, fearful about money, spending more than you earn and compulsive shopping are just a few of the signs that you have an unhealthy relationship with money. You are on the right path if you think in terms of the bigger picture by delaying gratification and not being fearful of money. Like with any other relationship in your life, you will need to dedicate time and attention if you want to improve it.

A checking account is different from a savings account, so do not treat them as one. A checking account typically earns minimal interest and keeps cash on hand to make withdrawals and to pay bills. In today's economy, a savings account earns very little interest due to low federal interest rates. A savings account is meant to hold money for a longer term or for a specific goal such as making a down payment on a car or home. Typically, banks charge a monthly maintenance fee for most checking accounts with balances under a certain threshold. However, plenty of banks do not charge this fee and offer a network of conveniently located ATMs. If you use ATMs often, this information is important for you to consider. ATMs that are out of your bank's network typically will charge a processing fee for each transaction. These fees, depending on how often you withdraw from an ATM, will add up quickly. So, to avoid these fees, look for banks that offer a large network of ATMs.

Understanding the difference between a *debit card* and a *credit card* is vitally important, as your payment responsibilities are different in each case. Briefly, a debit card is connected to a checking account where every swipe is like writing a check. On the other hand, a credit card allows the holder to purchase goods or services on credit, based on a contract signed with a bank. This difference will be explained fully in the next chapter.

The following list represents personal money management issues.

1. *Balance your checkbook each month.* This exercise is essential in managing your money. It allows you to find and correct any possible mistakes made during the month. By establishing this habit, balancing your checking account monthly becomes second nature. Getting into the habit of asking for ATM and debit card receipts for every transaction and recording them daily, will make the monthly balancing process much easier. Also, make sure all written checks and deposits are promptly written in your checkbook registry to provide you with a realistic, up to date financial picture. To stay organized, once you have recorded your transactions in your checkbook registry, place your receipts in labeled envelopes (label one envelope ATM Withdrawals, another Debit Card Swipes and the third Deposits). At the end of the month, balance your checkbook with the bank's monthly statement, and if there are any discrepancies, go through your receipts to resolve any issues. If you use a software

program, you can do this on your computer each month. It is very important to create this habit early in your life, since it is one of the most important life skills you need to acquire. Most bank staff are willing to sit down with you if you are doing this for the first time and will teach you how to balance your checkbook. It most likely will have to be at off hours when they are not super busy.

2. *How to set up a budget.* Creating a budget is key to financial success. If you do not know how much you are bringing in and how much you are spending, you could very well end up in the red (loss). That's when your financial problems begin. Getting into the habit of setting a budget, will help you reap financial rewards later in life. You might think setting up a monthly budget is complicated, but really it is not. First, determine your monthly *income* (how much net money you bring home). Next, you will have to add up your monthly *fixed expenses* (rent/mortgage payment, cell phone plan, home internet connection, car payment and car insurance), and finally, you will need to determine your *variable expenses* (groceries, electric, gas, water, household maintenance and entertainment). Variable expenses can change week to week, month to month, quarter to quarter and some depend on

your usage. For example, electricity payments might vary a bit depending on where you live and the season you are in. In the south, electricity consumption tends to be lower in the winter, due to less demand for air conditioning. In the north, it tends to be higher due to the demand for more heat.

On the next page is a <u>basic</u> and <u>simple</u> example of a monthly household budget. You may copy it or reproduce it in an excel spreadsheet.

JUNE

Household Budget	Monthly Income (+)	Monthly Expenses (-)
Take Home Pay 15th	$	
Take Home Pay 30th	$	
Mortgage or Rent		$
Gas/Oil		$
Electricity		$
Cell Phone		$
Cable/Internet		$
Car Loan & Insurance		$
Student Loan Debt		$
Credit Card Debt		$
Car Gasoline		$
Car Insurance		$
Commuting, parking (car misc.)		$
Groceries		$
Entertainment (dining, movies, etc.)		$
Clothing		$
Miscellaneous		$
Tithing (opt.)		$
Sub-totals	$	$

3. *Compare your expenses to your income.* Your subtotals are the additions of each column (income [+] - expenses [-] = disposable income). Your disposable income is the leftover monies that should be put into an emergency fund, a savings/investment account and then finally a vacation fund. An emergency fund is equal to about 3 to 9 months of your typical monthly expenses. Ideally, you should create a budget that allows you to save money each month, even if it is a minimal amount. By getting into this habit, you will undoubtedly increase your "rainy day fund." By comparing your expenses to your income, you begin to see exactly where your money is being spent. Financial literacy equals financial responsibility.

JUNE - Disposable Income

Monthly Leftover Monies	$	
Emergency Fund		$
Savings		$
Investment		$
Vacation Fund		$

4. *Track your expenses.* This is easy if you set up a system that you can follow. Again, here you can create categories by labeling some envelopes just as you did for balancing your checkbook. Budgeting software programs are available to track your expenses. So, ultimately it will all depend on your lifestyle. Remember, the key is to make it simple and easy for *you.* The envelope system worked for me. It organized and simplified the process of recording my expenses each week. By having a system in place, you might realize that you've overspent during the month of June, so you will cut back a bit in July.

5. *Discretionary spending.* These expenses are considered to be impulse purchases that in the end may not be necessary. Examples can include clothing items, apps and music downloads/CDs, DVDs, video games or electronic gadgets. Depending on your disposable income budget, which varies for everyone, you will determine your personal threshold of frivolous spending that makes you comfortable. Can you live without a daily Starbucks coffee? That's $5.00 per cup/day x 365 days (1 year) = $1,825.00. By choosing to

save $5 a day for one year, you will have saved enough money for a nice getaway.

6. *Adjust as necessary.* You will find that making financial adjustments are necessary throughout life. For example, your car may be in for a scheduled maintenance check-up and they find that your brake pads need replacing. Brake pads are expensive, so you will need to make an adjustment for the extra expense. This is why you have an emergency fund for issues that come up without warning.

7. *Evaluate your budget.* It's a good idea to evaluate your budget from time to time. As your life evolves with career changes, pay increases, marriage and children, it's a good idea to re-evaluate your budgetary needs. If you plan to purchase a car, make a down payment on a home or go on a vacation, you will need to set some long term financial goals. For example, if you receive a raise at work, you may choose to allocate those extra funds towards one of your financial goals. Periodically, evaluating your budget will enable you to see where adjustments are needed.

8. *Income Taxes.* An eventual rite of passage for many young adults is the requirement of the

Internal Revenue Service to file your income taxes. Filing your income taxes will teach you how the US tax system works and helps to create sound filing habits early in life. When you file your income taxes you will need your name and social security number along with W-2's (provided by your employer) or a 1099 if you are an independent contractor. Filing your taxes yearly is your responsibility and a critical part of your financial success. There are resources to assist you with filing your taxes so please seek them out.

Is Keeping Receipts Really Necessary?

Yes, for a variety of reasons. Certain receipts may be necessary for filing your income taxes. When you join a company and if you are required to submit an expense report, you must provide receipts, or you will not be reimbursed. This is especially important when traveling for business. In some cases, the company will issue their credit card for travel purposes, and you must ensure it is only used for company business.

Managing money successfully is a step by step process that is *your sole responsibility.* What would happen if you set out on a road trip without a map or a GPS? How would you know the direction you are going in? The same is true with your finances. Finances are one of the biggest issues couples argue about and many times can lead to the end of a relationship. Learning about and paying attention to financial matters for yourself will no doubt pave the way for you to talk about money openly.

Household Management

Household management combines time and money management strategies to assist you in developing and creating your unique lifestyle. Visualize yourself living in a beautiful apartment that is clean and organized, with a well-stocked kitchen where you are ready to entertain friends. You always have fresh clean laundry and a feeling of financial security. Yes, this is *all* possible for you. Successful *time*, *money* and *household management* are all about creating routines that develop *good personal habits* for a lifetime.

1. *Shopping for everyday essentials.* Once you are living independently of your parents, the responsibility for ensuring that you never run out of toilet paper falls solely on you. Look for sales to save wherever you can, as many grocery stores have BOGO (buy one get one free) items on a weekly basis and usually publish a weekly flyer of their sale items. For example, with some comparison shopping, you will quickly learn that paper towels, toilet paper and toiletries are better priced at different stores. Farmer's markets are also great places to shop, and you'll be helping local small business farmers. Get into the habit of creating a grocery list. When you determine your

toilet paper supply is running low, begin your list. As you run low on other supplies, add those things to your list and before you know it, you'll have a grocery list. After a quick check of the pantry and refrigerator, you can add items to your list if necessary. Now you are ready to go grocery shopping.

2. *Learn to plan for meals, prepare, cook and store leftovers.* If you have never cooked before, you might be pleasantly surprised that cooking is an art form. By planning your meals for the week, it makes it easier when coming home at night from work. In the frozen section of your grocery store, there are a tremendous variety of simple meals you can choose from. If preparing meals from scratch, get a simple cookbook, read the directions and you just might surprise yourself. Also, you might enjoy entertaining your friends with a meal. Practice makes perfect when it comes to cooking from scratch so, enjoy it. It's fun!

3. *Doing laundry.* Learning to do laundry can be confusing at first, but it is simple once you understand how to do it. Read the washing instruction labels for new clothing items. This is very important and a good rule of thumb, as new clothing that has never been washed before might

color bleed or shrink if not washed per the instructions. Once you have all the dirty laundry out, make sure to check that all the pockets are empty. Next, sort the clothing into three different piles. Whites, light and pastels, and the dark colors such as navy blue, browns and even dark reds. Some labels have special instructions, such as *hand wash* or *cold water only* and should have their own piles. Towels, bed linens and kitchen towels, depending on their colors, can be washed together.

If you have any clothing items with stains, pre-treat with a stain remover then place them in the machine. In general, whites should be washed in warm or hot water and colors, including light or dark should be washed in cold water. Remember, washing any items in *hot water* over time will eventually cause shrinkage. When in doubt about any clothing, use cold water. Open the washer lid and add the detergent first. With today's easy to use POD detergents, messy measuring cups are no longer needed. Place the clothes evenly in the washer in a circular manner and close the lid. Select the appropriate wash cycle setting and water temperature then press the start button. Depending on the wash cycle, it can take between 30 to 45 minutes to complete.

After the clothes are washed, remove them and shake them out before placing in the dryer. This will ensure they dry quicker with less wrinkles. Before placing your clothes in the dryer, make sure to always check the lint screen, as this can cause a fire if clogged. Once clothes are in the dryer, set the timer and temperature, and before you know it, you've done your laundry. As soon as your clothes are dry, hang them up for minimal wrinkles and fold all the other items.

4. *Keeping a clean and tidy home.* One of the best habits to teach yourself is to make your bed every day. As soon as your bed is made, the room will look and feel organized, and it only takes a minute. In the bathroom, after you shower and dry yourself, hang up the towel so it air dries. As soon as you use toothpaste or other toiletries, put them back where they belong. Once you are done in the bathroom, give the counter a quick wipe. A great tip is "If you take it out, put it back." This tip will ensure to keep things organized and tidy.

In the kitchen, make a habit of loading the dishwasher as soon as you finish eating and then wipe the counters. Run the dishwasher only when it is full. If you run the dishwasher at night, empty it out the next morning. It will only take a few minutes. Once you get into the habit of doing a little something every day, before you know it, you have created routines and habits to be proud of. There are many products on the market today, so you have lots of choices that make cleaning easy and efficient. Go visit your local grocery store or big box stores and peruse the cleaning aisles. Look for items that are efficient and easy to use.

5. *Miscellaneous.* It's a good idea to create a couple of basic tool kits for your home. Without a doubt, you will need them at some point in your life. The first should be a tool kit that incorporates items you will need for your apartment or home. Items for your basic "home tool kit" should include a tape measure, a hammer and nails, pliers and a multi-purpose screwdriver. Adding a roll of duct tape is also a good idea because of its versatile uses. The tape measure will come in handy to measure any kind of project around your home such as wall hangings. If you are shopping for a piece of furniture, first measure the space to ensure the item will fit, so there won't be any surprises. Believe me at some point, the

screwdriver, pliers, hammer and nails will also come in handy. As the need arises for additional items, simply purchase what you require. The second kit is a "first aid kit" filled with everything necessary for any cuts, scrapes or bruises. First aid kits are readily available in most stores or can be purchased online. These are the kinds of things we don't think about when first starting out. They will save you time and are essential to have in every home.

6. *Negotiate large purchases.* When purchasing a new or used car, research and information are vital keys in negotiating a fair price. Know in advance what you can afford. Getting pre-approved for a loan before you begin the search, can help you avoid time spent shopping for cars you can't afford. Once you have your pre-approval, you should have a ballpark figure of what you can afford. This applies to all cars, new, used or certified used. Many people go into a car dealership looking to buy a car, and their only concern is the monthly payment.

If you inform the sales person up front about your monthly budget figure, *you cannot negotiate a price. I cannot stress how important this is.* A successful negotiating strategy should begin by informing the sales person that you have done some homework on the desired make, model and options. Then, from that starting point, the sales person likely will ask, "What is your monthly budget?" Sales people are trained to ask this question *multiple times* during the conversation. So, be prepared to dodge this question with a smile. Negotiating is like a poker game; always show your poker face, and never give away your figures. Since you have a ballpark figure of what you can afford, look for cars in that general price range.

Once you have found a car to your liking, ask the salesperson, "How much are you willing to take off the list price?" *Never pay sticker price!* It is a simple question, which they will answer with, "There is very little room for negotiation." Keep in mind this is a trained response. The key here is for the sales person to make the first discount offer. That way you can counter and come in with a lower figure. For example, if the sales person comes in with an original discount of $2000.00, you might consider coming back with an additional discount of $2000.00 or $3000.00.

Being prepared to walk away from any deal gives *you, the customer,* all the power. There are many new and used car dealers, large and small that sell a tremendous number of vehicles each month. Once you have negotiated a final price, you might surprise yourself to find that your budgeted, monthly payment is lower than your initial expectation. *Certified used cars* are sold by dealerships. The term certified used car means the dealership has conducted an overall inspection of the car to prepare it for sale and it can come with or without a warranty. When purchasing a used car from a private individual, do not rely on what the person is telling you about the condition of the car, no matter how cool the vehicle appears. *Remember they want to sell their car.*

I highly recommend you hire a good mechanic to inspect the vehicle before purchasing. This investment will provide you peace of mind and may save you thousands of dollars in future repair costs. Kelly Blue Book and Edmunds are two excellent sources of everything automotive. Get these free apps and use them to your advantage. *Remember, the bottom line is, everything is negotiable, everything!*

7. *Car Insurance.* An insurance payment will be higher on a new model versus a similar used car. By shopping around and getting multiple rate

quotes, you may be able to apply any savings to a greater down payment.

8. *Car Maintenance.* A little money spent on regular maintenance goes a long way. This is essential to keeping your car in tip-top shape and avoiding major repairs as well as frustrating, dangerous situations. Having a tire pressure gauge and checking your tires (including your spare) monthly and before a long trip, you will not only get better gas mileage but avoid a possible blow-out due to an overheated, under-inflated tire. If you are unsure of the proper tire pressure for your car, check the label inside the driver's door. Countless times I have witnessed people of all ages stranded on the side of the highway due to a flat tire. If checking your tire pressure seems too much for you, ask a friend or visit an automotive shop for some assistance.

An oil change is another essential element in keeping your car running in peak condition. Depending on your environmental conditions, an oil change is usually done every 3000 to 5000 miles. If you live in a four-season environment, with less than ideal air quality, your oil will tend to get dirty faster. If this is the case, you should have your oil changed every 3000 miles. On the contrary, if you live in a mild climate with no harsh driving conditions, you could stretch that figure to 5000 miles, saving you some money. The company doing the oil change usually puts a reminder sticker for the next oil change in the upper left-hand corner of the windshield. Additionally, don't ignore odd sounding noises, as your car is trying to tell you something. Dash warning lights, even if they go away temporarily, should not be ignored, since they are there to warn you about something. If you ignore them, it could prove to be an expensive lesson. Another important element of your car's maintenance is the brakes. Depending on your driving habits and environmental conditions, your brakes may need to be replaced more often. Regularly scheduled, general maintenance will ensure that your car is always running in peak condition.

Keep in mind that your household management will evolve over time. You and only you are responsible for your home environment and the lifestyle that you choose to live.

Roommates, Lease Agreements/Contracts

One day, you might consider whether to have a roommate. There are advantages and disadvantages. An advantage of having a roommate is the ability to split the cost of rent and utility payments. It provides the opportunity to rent a larger apartment versus living on your own. You may also split the costs of shared items such as toiletries and groceries. Additionally, they'll keep you company, increase your social skills, teach you to compromise and share responsibilities. A significant disadvantage could be a failure to pay their share of the rent on time. Losing your privacy, messiness and not living up to shared responsibilities should also be considered. The bottom line is that having a roommate can be an enriching experience if properly vetted. I will go into more detail in the next section to assist in the vetting process.

Another important consideration will be the lease agreement. Should you sign it alone or with your roommate? First, you will need to check with the landlord if they will allow you to have a roommate that is not listed on the lease agreement. Some landlords will not allow for a roommate unless their name is included on the lease. A joint lease agreement requires the signature of both parties. If you sign the lease in your name only, then you are solely responsible for making the monthly rent payment. Before you sign any lease agreement, you must clearly understand the consequences of breaking the contract, as you will be held liable. Some landlords could hold you responsible for the entire lease agreement. Other landlords may allow you the opportunity to find someone else to take over the lease, if they qualify. In most cases, if you break the lease, you lose the deposit money.

When signing a contract, it is essential to *read it before signing on the dotted line.* Yes, I know some contracts are long and cumbersome, contain lots of legalese jargon and can be difficult to understand. All that jargon is there for a reason. For example, when leasing a car, there are a certain number of miles that you are allowed per year. If you go over that mileage allowance, then you pay a penalty fee for each mile after that.

Be aware that a credit check will be conducted on everyone involved in the lease agreement. This is very important, as you can be denied through no fault of your own if your potential roommate has a low credit score. Before negotiating any lease, addressing this issue with a likely roommate is vital to your success in being approved.

In any contract, legal agreement or lease, be aware that your *credit score* will have a major impact on the terms of the agreement. In Chapter 7 "Credit Cards, Debt & Fico Scores," I will cover your *credit score* and what it means. Before signing on the dotted line, please be sure that you clearly understand the consequences if you are unable to live up to the agreed upon terms. *Read the fine print.*

During my early life as a single person, having a roommate enabled me to live in a larger apartment that I could not have afforded on my own. What was not clear to me at the time was the impact a roommate would make on my day to day life. In addition to being neat and tidy, my humble home had always been my haven from the outside world.

My first experience with a roommate was with a fellow flight attendant in a small studio apartment in NYC. With no prior references to vouch for our financial ability to pay the rent on time, the landlord required a deposit equaling six month's rent. When we first started out as roommates, everything was good. Since our schedules were different, except for a few times, we had the tiny studio apartment mostly to ourselves. The efforts I took to clean up and leave the apartment neatly arranged and ordered were not matched by my roommate. On many occasions, I came home from a long trip to find dirty dishes in the sink and her clothes strewn about the apartment.

After five months of living together, a fellow flight attendant mentioned to me that my roommate had intentions of moving back to her home state of Florida. When I asked her the same question, she assured me she was not moving. Since together we had signed a one-year lease agreement, I had to believe her. Well, at the end of six months, she moved out while I was away on a trip.

Feeling betrayed by her dishonesty and now fully responsible for the monthly rent until I could find a new roommate, I took action and changed the locks on the apartment. Upon returning home from a four-day trip abroad, the superintendent of the building told me she had made an unsuccessful attempt to gain entry into my apartment. Additionally, I learned from the landlord that she had also made an unsuccessful attempt to get her deposit money refunded. The consequence of breaking her contractual part of the lease agreement was losing her three month's deposit. It is important to understand the consequences of signing any type of lease agreement or contract.

Questions for Prospective Roommates

What do you do for a living? If they have a completely different work schedule, consider it a good thing. Being on different work schedules provides some much-needed time alone in your apartment. Do they have the ability to work from home, and if so, how often do they choose to do this? Learning as much as you can about what they do for a living, will provide a clearer picture of what to expect.

How often do you clean? Listen carefully to how they answer this question. It is not the same as asking them are you a clean person? No one will admit to being a messy slob. Ask them what household chores they like to do and share your habits with them. Honesty is the key here since many roommate disputes and conflicts often involve organization and cleanliness.

Do you smoke? It seems like an obvious question if you are a non-smoker. However, you must also be aware that some landlords and lease agreements forbid smoking inside. If they are an occasional smoker, ask them what do they mean by occasional?

What time do you usually go to bed? If you are a light sleeper and in bed by 11 pm, and they are a night owl up until the wee hours with music playing, they may not be a good roommate match for you. Other people's late-night habits, if very different from yours, will affect you.

What kind of music do you listen to? Will it create a conflict if you like to blast heavy metal and they enjoy listening to pop music? This is just another piece to be aware of in the roommate puzzle.

Do you expect out of town visitors, and how long do they usually stay? Vital for you to know so you can establish rules and expectations. A weekend visit may be okay, but a longer stay may create a crowding issue.

Do you have any pets? Are you considering getting a pet? If your lease agreement does not allow for pets, you must inform them. If your lease agreement allows for pets, you must ask these questions, since it is impossible to read their minds.

Do you cook and how often? If both of you like to cook, the kitchen will undoubtedly be crowded. On the other hand, if one cooks and the other does not, it might be a good match. Then, the question is who will clean up? Set up ground rules and expectations to avoid coming home to an empty fridge and dirty kitchen.

What is your romantic situation? Learning about each other's romantic situation may bring more people into the mix. It is essential to set boundaries for both parties regarding significant others.

What do you like to do on weekends? Do you prefer to socialize at home or outside the house? These questions are not about judging, they simply allow you to learn about the prospective roommate. Ultimately, it will be up to both of you to negotiate and compromise while meshing your lifestyles.

Do you have references? Just like in a job interview, roommate references are important. If they don't have any, then ask for two or three names of co-workers, as they too can provide some insight. Ask for their phone numbers and email information.

Can you put a deposit down? By asking this question, it will help you to assess their financial situation. This question may not even apply if you are signing a joint lease agreement, as a deposit *will be* required from both of you. Remember the roommate who broke her lease agreement and moved out without prior notice. She made an unsuccessful attempt to collect her deposit money from the landlord without my knowledge. Since we had a signed joint lease agreement, she simply forfeited her money, and I became solely responsible for the rent.

What do you want in a roommate? Just as you would like answers to questions, they also need to learn about you. This question provides them with the opportunity to voice something that perhaps was not covered in the conversation. During the back and forth dialogue, you will get an idea if this person is a good match. It can summarize if you are on the same page.

Is there anything else you would like to add?
Is there anything additional I can answer for you?

If at any time during this process, you find they are not a good fit, just end the interview politely. If they end it, then you will know you are not what they were looking for in a roommate. *Do not take it personally!* It will save you lots of headaches and frustrations and leave an opening for the person *who is the right fit.*

Chapter 7

Credit Cards, Debt & FICO Scores

Avoid long-term credit card debt at all costs. Learning the difference between a credit card and a debit card is extremely important. As I explained earlier in this book, a debit card is attached to a bank account and every transaction you make is immediately (within 24 hours) deducted from your account. When using a debit card, you are in fact paying cash for your items or services. It does not feel like you are using cash to spend money when you simply swipe a plastic card through a machine. This is why in the earlier money management chapter I stressed the importance of keeping debit card receipts.

Try the following exercise to experience the emotional difference between spending cold, hard cash versus using a plastic debit card. With a total budget of $100.00, imagine spending $50.00 using cash and the other $50.00 using your debit card. Which method of payment appeared to make the greatest financial impact on you, and which one was easier to use? Did you think twice about spending the cash versus using the debit card? Sometimes we treat items in life with greater care when they represent a real and tangible value. Plastic is plastic and has no direct tangible value unless attached to something. Did you have a greater emotional attachment to the cash?

On the other hand, a credit card allows you to spend more money than you have *for a price*. That price is called an interest rate. Don't charge money on your credit card that you cannot afford to pay off at the end of each month. You must clearly understand credit card interest rates, before you sign on the dotted line of the application. Shop around to find the lowest annual interest rate. You will find stores that offer 10% off your first purchase, if you open a credit card with them. Sometimes these store promotions are used as a marketing gimmick to get you into a high annual interest rate credit card. Do not fall victim to these kinds of sales promotions.

When it comes to your money, knowledge and information are very powerful. Always read the fine print which will include the credit card *"annual percentage interest rate"* known as the APR. Banks are in the business of making money. A low APR is great for the consumer but bad for a bank's profits. For example, if you do not pay off your entire monthly balance (not the minimum payment), the APR will kick in for all future bills until the balance is paid off. This could add a significant cost to you each month, depending on your balance. If you choose to pay the minimum amount each month, it could result in convincing yourself, "I can afford more by simply paying the minimum monthly amount." Before you know it, your credit card is maxed out and you have fallen victim to the credit card debt trap, racking up thousands of dollars of debt, which is the worst kind of debt to acquire.

The whole point of this is for you to understand, that living beyond your means is financially self-destructive. Many people are unwilling to delay gratification, which is "I want it now" thinking. Most of us, at some point in our lives, need to make large purchases on our credit cards. My emphasis to you is pay-off the large purchases quickly, before adding another additional large purchase. Banks and retailers will always entice you to open a new credit card account. Don't do it! Do your research first. You will be happy you did.

Following is an example of an APR and what compounding interest means. Let's say you charge $100.00 on your credit card. The monthly statement you receive might state that the minimum payment due is $15.00. If you choose to pay the minimum amount, you might think $85.00 is all you owe. Think again, next month's statement balance adds the bank interest rate to the $85.00. So, depending on this interest rate, you may now owe $92.00 on next month's statement. Seven dollars may not seem like a lot however, the compounding interest adds up quickly. Banks usually charge credit card interest on a compounded, daily basis for maximum profits. This daily compounded interest figure will be very small and appear to be insignificant. For example, a bank may advertise a "daily interest rate of 0.041%," which seems low but after multiplying it by 365 (days/year) will equal an APR of (14.965%) or 15%. So, when shopping around for a credit card, do your homework and make sure to compare annual percentage rates.

Credit card debt has some of the highest interest rates out there, meaning it is the worst kind of debt for you to take on so early in your life.

Banks will tell you it is never too early to build or establish your credit score. This is your record of financial trustworthiness and while this is true, you must exercise extreme discipline when it comes to using a credit card. Planning and budgeting for a large purchase on your credit card is not always possible. When you find yourself in this situation, create a new budget to pay off the item as soon as possible. The easiest way to get yourself into a financial disaster is to carry a large balance on your credit card. It is easy to use a rectangular piece of plastic daily. By getting a Starbucks coffee in the morning, another in the afternoon and for lunch swiping the card again at Panera's, you will have spent an easy $20.00 or more. When you add up $20.00 five days a week for four weeks, you are looking at $400.00 a month of your gross income. A medium Café Vanilla Frappuccino at Starbucks costs $5.04 including tax. If you have a Frappuccino four days a week, in one year you will have spent just under $1050.00. Cut your consumption by two, and you can save approximately $525.00.

Building your credit score is extremely important for you to fully understand. You begin to build your credit score by paying the rent, electric, gas and cell phone bills on time each month. All your debt must be paid in a timely manner. Most landlords and companies have a given grace period for the payment to be considered an "on-time payment" (usually, within a certain number of days of the due date). *If you are late or miss just one payment, your credit score will be negatively affected.* With today's technology, automatic bank deductions make it easy to pay your bills on time every month.

Another method used in building your credit score is through a secured credit card. On the surface, a secured credit card appears to offer the same convenience as a regular credit card by providing you access to a credit line. In this instance, the credit line is funded by a security deposit you first make to the bank in an amount equal to your maximum total purchase limit. This tool is used primarily to establish or repair a credit history, as your payment activity will be reported to the major credit bureaus. Use it to purchase items, make payments and if you carry a balance, an interest rate will apply.

A secured credit card is not meant to be used forever. It is intended to help establish your credit worthiness. Choose a secured credit card that has no fees or a low annual fee. Make sure the bank reports to all three credit bureaus, so you are building your credit trustworthiness.

FICO Scores

Like social security numbers, most of us have a FICO score. A FICO score is a type of credit rating that lenders use to assess the applicant's credit risk and whether to extend a loan. It is the score that determines the likelihood of the person paying their debts. The generic FICO score is between 300 and 850. The higher the FICO score, the better.

The three credit bureaus are Equifax, Experian and TransUnion. Credit bureaus are companies that collect information related to the credit rating of individuals. They make the information available to credit card institutions and banks for them to determine your credit risk.

Every time a lender accesses your credit record your credit score declines, so it is necessary to maintain a solid credit report. A "good" credit (670-739) score comes from paying your bills off in a timely manner. This is how over time you raise your credit score which provides access to more credit at better interest rates. Aim for a "very good" credit (740-799) so that your score can sustain the decline that comes with lender inquiries.

Credit scores are central to your financial life, and it is important for you to know that they don't always get it right. Should you ever find discrepancies in your credit report, make sure to document your correspondence with the agency properly. Having experienced this scenario myself, I learned that you will also need lots of patience.

Learn how to check your credit report and FICO score to ensure the information is accurate. Check out myfico.com to learn what is in a FICO score and what data is used to determine that number.

Chapter 8

Apprenticeship and Internship Programs

Apprenticeships and internships both provide you with hands-on training, and that is where the similarities end. Today, some employers are trying to appeal to a younger generation by creating an early version of internships for high school graduates. Your current generation has a tremendous amount of available opportunities.

Internships are usually for someone who is attending college and may be paid or unpaid. Internships provide a way to *explore different kinds of careers and job opportunities* and can benefit people who are unsure of what they would like to pursue in life. For many students in varying programs, completing an internship is a graduation requirement. Often, a company who hires interns has a special project in mind and looks for a certain skill set in their candidates. These internships last for a specific period of time.

Summer internships are popular with average durations of eight to ten weeks over the student's break from school. Since most interns are not college seniors, after completing their internships, companies understand they will return to school to continue with their studies. Remember internships are available throughout your college career, and as stated earlier, are a way to explore different job opportunities. Upon graduation, it is also possible to land a full-time position through an internship, if it is a good match.

Apprenticeships are for *someone who knows what type of job or career they want* and has obtained a high school diploma or GED Certificate. Almost always, an apprentice earns money while they learn the trade or craft, working side by side with an expert employee. The company expects that the apprentice will work for them as a full-time employee after the apprenticeship is completed.

Apprenticeship programs have long existed in Europe and are on the rise in the United States. America needs a new generation of workers for particular trades and professions, hence the reason for the rise in these programs. Apprenticeship programs used to focus primarily on the manual labor industry, such as automotive repair, carpentry and electrical, but with today's advances in technology, there are ample opportunities beyond the labor industry. Upon completion of many programs, participants obtain a license or a professional certification and will become a full-time employee. Some certifications are equivalent to an associate degree, which can provide a path to a higher education. Here are three reasons to consider an apprenticeship program.

1. *You begin earning money.* Apprenticeships allow you to earn as you learn, unlike a traditional educational path where you pay to learn your skill. Some classroom instruction might also be required.
2. *Options galore.* There is a wealth of options when it comes to apprenticeship opportunities. Today, apprenticeship programs can include roles in sales, marketing and operations.
3. *Less time than you think.* Depending on your chosen field, an apprenticeship program can last one to four years, perhaps more. The key to remember is that you are earning while you are learning.

If you know what kind of job or career you desire, then finding the right apprenticeship program is essential. Following are some additional considerations in lieu of the traditional four-year degree.

- What kinds of skills are you interested in learning?
- What programs are being offered in your geographic area?
- Are you willing to move if your area does not offer the right program?
- How long does the program take?

Apprenticeship programs are not the easy way out; therefore, you must be genuinely interested in what you are learning. When you are chosen for an apprenticeship program, the company is investing money – lots of money in you. Like any investment, the company wants an ROI, what is known in the business world as a return on investment. When you have a burning desire to add value to an organization, they too will be committed to your success.

How does one go about finding an apprenticeship program? If you are still in high school, a guidance counselor can help get you started. On the other hand, if you are a high school graduate or have obtained a GED certificate, then you will need to research what opportunities are available.

Determination and perseverance will become your best friends.

On the Florida Department of Education website is a "General Information Sheet on Apprenticeships" that may be useful to you. Here is the link: http://www.fldoe.org/core/fileparse.php/3/urlt/general -apprenticeship-information.pdf

The United States Department of Labor link for Apprenticeships is: https://www.dol.gov/apprenticeship/

There is an additional link with contact information where all the state Apprenticeship USA offices are listed. Here is the link: https://doleta.gov/oa/stateoffices.cfm#GA

This federal link provides the name of the state contact, their business address, phone number and email. By carefully exploring this link, you may discover opportunities once thought impossible to you. Make sure to carefully review all the categories listed in the column on the left side of the website. In addition, the following link https://doleta.gov/OA/regdirlist.cfm connects to the six regional offices across the country of Apprenticeship USA. There you will find, the Regional Director's name, address, phone number and email along with the territory they are responsible for managing.

Another comprehensive website sponsored by the Department of Labor is https://www.careeronestop.org

Here you can explore careers, find training opportunities, conduct job searches and find an abundance of additional resources to assist you. Career One Stop is partnered with American Job Network. For those of you who have a great social network, they will show you how to leverage those contacts. This website is an excellent resource that has offices around the country.

Chapter 9

Social Media Responsibility

Today's graduates impress me with their potential and capabilities for being strong, innovative leaders, looking to change the world for the better. Their creativity, imagination and original ideas set that generation apart from the Baby Boomers, Generation Xers and Millennials of the world.

Today more than ever, your online social media profile and presence matter. While many use social media to connect and share with friends and family, there are others who use it to create funny videos, provoking laughter and some even move us to tears. Some social media sharing and posting pictures and videos are appropriate, while others are not. Many of us from different generations have benefited immensely from the internet. Today's generation has been encouraged to share and post *everything* online about their lives, as a way to connect with others. These postings can lead to unintended consequences.

Please know that I get it. You don't want anyone telling you what to do and much less what not to do. So, before you use your smartphone to share or post something with the world, I want you to avoid damaging your online reputations. A simple **think before you post** is my recommendation because the internet is an enormous public record. Once on the internet, it is usually a permanent record and never entirely deleted.

Today employers and schools alike are checking social media networks before they grant an interview. It is never too early to make adjustments to your online profile. Here are a few quick and easy first steps in making sure your online presence is everything you want it to be.

- As obvious as it may seem, remove any pictures or posts that can be perceived to be unfavorable. Also, look for posts that you were tagged in and remove them if they are uncomplimentary.
- Privatize your social network accounts, so you know exactly what the world sees regarding your

accounts. Privacy policies change from time to time, so it is important to stay on top of the changes.

- Emphasize the good stuff you have achieved. If you have participated in community service or volunteered your time, make sure to write about it on your social media networks.

Your online reputation is just as important as your personal reputation. Make sure to protect it!

Carmen Topper

Chapter 10

Self-Empowerment

How do you eat an entire elephant? *One bite at a time!* This analogy also applies to the process of self-empowerment, which relates to the knowledge you gain about the "self" and how to use it to further your dreams, desires and goals. It is a process that continues to evolve over a lifetime.

Self-empowerment involves taking *full responsibility* for your life and all the choices you make along the way. Living a self-empowered life is both liberating and scary at the same time. Liberating because it means you are fully accountable and responsible for everything in your life. Everything! Scary because there is no one to blame for any choices or decisions you *choose* to make. Please do not take my words out of context. If someone ran a red light and caused an accident, then there is someone to blame. I refer to personal choices we make that produce direct results in our life.

Self-empowerment requires you to examine your emotional self and its behaviors. The ability to understand your own emotions and their effects on all areas of your life is dependent on you alone. When you can better understand your feelings and why they appear at times to be so strong, you will further your efforts in developing your self-empowerment abilities.

Consider and think about the following questions designed to help you reflect on the person you are in life. Be honest about your responses. Authenticity is one of the key elements to self-empowerment.

- Are you blaming others for negative events in your life and why?
- Are you giving yourself excuses, and if so, what are you avoiding?
- Are you a victim of something? You may not even notice that you've adopted a victim mentality because of something that happened long ago.
- Are you looking for attention and sympathy from others? Being a victim sometimes feels

good because it brings concern and caring from others.

- What story are you telling yourself and others? Listen to the narrative you describe to others regarding your life.

- Who and what are you blaming? The story we tell ourselves and others is what we are consistently creating in our lives.

- Why is this or that not possible for you? Why did it happen to me?

Those questions were not meant to think about for a long time rather for you to reflect and recognize possible patterns in your life. Once you become aware of a possible event, situation or way of being that is unsatisfactory then the window of opportunity opens to create a different outcome. Without awareness, change is not possible.

Being self-empowered means, we have the personal knowledge, awareness and belief in ourselves to create the life we choose. Many of us are unaware of how powerful our word choices can be during everyday conversation. The words we choose to communicate with others about ourselves are more powerful than you can imagine. Expand your everyday vocabulary and use powerful, dynamic and effective words whenever possible.

Self-empowerment is about
believing in you and taking action!

If you are not a self-confident or self-assured person, you can begin by creating daily habits that build confidence. When things get tough in life, and they will, empowering yourself is the one thing that will enable you to move in a forward direction. The tough times we all face in life can be viewed in two distinct ways. First, is to feel that we are defeated or that it wasn't meant to be or that we failed. Second, is to consider it a set up for something greater in your life. Everyone faces difficult and challenging times. You are no different. Believe it or not, those times are meant for your good, since life is ten percent what happens to us and ninety percent how we respond.

You are destined to leave your mark on this world. Don't let anyone discourage your efforts. The special talents and gifts that you were born with are uniquely yours. They simply cannot be replicated.

The process of empowerment happens as you become stronger and more confident in all areas of your life. Even when you've experienced a tough time or failed at something, choose to consider the results as an outcome of your efforts. The outcome was not what you initially set out to achieve; nevertheless, it was an outcome. As children, many of us worked with puzzles. Have you ever tried inserting a puzzle piece and it did not fit? Inserting the puzzle piece in the wrong area produced a result – it did not fit. Since it was not the desired result, you went on to choose another puzzle piece. You didn't beat yourself up because you chose the wrong puzzle piece but just tried again with a different puzzle piece. If that piece didn't fit, you continued to look for the missing piece until you found a fit. The "puzzle piece" analogy can be used interchangeably to describe your experiences in the world of technology. Perhaps for you, the "puzzle piece" was Pokémon Go or a video game such as The Legend of Zelda that required an understanding of what was necessary to achieve success. It is likely, you became proficient at the game by playing it often.

"If at first you don't succeed, then try, try again." Thomas H. Palmer

Always remember you never fail until you give up!

One of my favorite authors and from whom I learned much in my life was Dr. Wayne Dyer. He said, "If you change the way you look at things, the things you look at change." Please stop for a moment and re-read the quote.

Self-knowledge is very important to the self-empowerment puzzle piece of your life. When you feel empowered, there is a sense of feeling that you control your life by the choices you make. It is a lifelong process, and as your knowledge and experiences increase, you also build on the strengths necessary to move forward in the direction of your goals.

Do you recall a time in your life when you were all fired up about some project or goal and yet still doubted you have what it takes? Was there a person whose words of encouragement such as *"Of course you can do it, I can see you doing it,"* instantaneously magnified your confidence? If you can relate to this scenario, you have a direct experience of feeling empowered. What if that friend or mentor were not there encouraging you? What can *you* do to put an end to the self-doubt and feel a lasting sense of empowerment?

There are a variety of things to do each day to increase your sense of empowerment. These things are called *habits.* Your life is shaped by the habits you choose to create and cultivate. It is *what* you repeatedly do over time that defines your success in every area of life. Additionally, your habits influence your self-confidence, level of motivation, your view of the future and your well-being. By choosing good habits, you will dramatically improve your life. Whereas, by choosing bad habits, you will interrupt the flow, possibly slowing you down or preventing you from accomplishing your goals. It is always a *choice*.

Generating change within yourself and knowing that it is possible for you is where you begin. *Trusting yourself* is the starting point.

Resist the habit of comparing yourself to others.

You came into this world with your own set of unique talents, along with everything else necessary to create and achieve a successful and happy life. Success and happiness are subjective and a matter of perspective. If you notice you are further behind someone else, or not in the career position of a friend, then you are comparing yourself to others. Maybe you look at how many friends others have on Facebook and think, "I don't have that many friends." Or, maybe someone has more LinkedIn connections or Twitter followers than you. Whatever it is, when you compare yourself to others, you are looking at yourself through the **insecurity and judgment filter**. All of us have filters that we use to view ourselves and others. These filters primarily come from the environment we grew up in and include our family members, some of our teachers and even our friends.

Self-empowerment comes from within. So, when you resist comparing yourself to others, you are engaging the power of your mind to create the changes you desire in your life. The moment you notice that you're beginning to compare yourself, immediately *stop* that train of thought and refocus the mind. Free yourself from the anxiety of living up to the social expectations of others. When you stop living up to other people's social expectations of you, it'll be the moment you'll find freedom. Obviously, there are certain family, work and social responsibilities that must be met. My point here is for you to find freedom from what others "think" of you. People will always have a good or bad opinion of you. Do not let what others think of you affect the core of who you are. You are a unique individual brought into this world to make a difference.

Here is an easy exercise to refocus the mind and build confidence. You will need a few 3 x 5 cards and a pen, or you can use your notepad app on a smartphone. Take a few minutes to reflect, recognize and acknowledge your unique talents and gifts. Make a list of these talents and gifts and write them on the 3 x 5 cards or the notepad app on your phone. If you are unsure of what your special talents include, consider asking someone in your life, who encouraged and supported you in the past. If using the cards, place them in different areas of your surroundings that are easily accessible and refer to them often. Put one on your nightstand, another in a drawer at your workplace and another in your car. Whichever method you choose, by having them readily accessible, they will remind you to refocus your mind on the unique capabilities that only you have to offer. Again, the key here is to ensure you are viewing them consistently throughout your day. A consistent visual reminder such as the cards will help to strengthen your motivation and belief in yourself. This is more empowering than the distracting self-judgments and negative self-talk you tell yourself. Refer to the cards or notepad app often, and over time your self-confidence will strengthen and increase.

During your lifetime, you will have setbacks, who doesn't? The key is not to let them set you back too far, so that you might completely give up on your dreams, desires and goals. *Never – give up – never!* Learn from the setbacks. Remember, the setback can be a "set-up" for your next success! You never fail until you give up!

All of us have "an automatic response system" that we have learned throughout our lives. In many cases, the automatic response system can be extremely critical of simple mistakes we've made. All of us make mistakes and forgiving ourselves is a critical building block to living a life of self-empowerment. Appreciate what you have already accomplished in life. You may think, "I have not really accomplished much in my life." That is a clear example of the negative self-talk and the kind of judgment that does not serve us well. Learn to appreciate even the smallest of accomplishments in your life, as this awareness and gratitude will strengthen your sense of empowerment.

Taking responsibility for the choices we make is a key element to feeling a sense of empowerment. Many of us leave our choices and decisions to *chance,* and then we complain about the outcome. When we make *some* choices in life, most of us do so with the information we have on hand and expect a positive result. Perhaps, we never consider that we don't have all the information we need to make a particular decision.

Then something goes wrong, and the result is not what we envisioned or expected. We are disappointed with ourselves and delve into self-pity and self-doubt by listening to the internal voices that speak loudly into our consciousness. *The truth here is that you will make some choices in life which do not turn out as expected.* Winners do not allow self-doubt, discouragement and negative self-talk to triumph. Alternatively, you can use this as a starting point to begin again with a renewed sense of empowerment and motivation.

Some of the choices I've made in my life did not turn out as expected. What became clear to me over time was that those choices were not the correct decisions. The result of taking the particular risk or gamble and not allowing fate to dictate the outcome of the situation, always led to more personal growth. Personal growth is about our evolution as an individual. Sometimes personal growth feels enormously exhilarating, and other times you might believe it is unbearable. Keep in mind that using the words "feel and believe" are a subjective impression.

Remember, we experience life through the lenses of our own good and bad experiences. There were many "gut check" times in my life and all resulted from right and wrong choices. Gut check is an evaluation of your resolve or commitment to something. Typically, when we make the wrong choice, we instinctively go back in our mind and gut check ourselves. So, in reflecting on an experience, we may realize that we've missed something. Hopefully, we've learned from it and move ahead.

So, when do you listen to your gut instinct? Instinct is one of your greatest internal resources and while it is invaluable, it is not infallible. When you practice going with "your gut," it requires you to be more instinctive. Understanding your emotional self is part of the learning that needs to happen in order to trust your gut. Give yourself the mental space by taking time to reflect on events, meetings and situations in your life. This time alone with yourself will help you to develop an awareness of how you feel in certain situations and will strengthen your instincts. *Your instinct can only be developed by you.* Being instinctive is not a natural trait. It is an aspect of ourselves that increases or decreases, given the amount of practice dedicated to it. Like many things in life, the more you practice, the better you become.

Let's use a job interview as an example. Some individuals might feel nervous when first meeting the interviewer. They may or may not make us feel welcome or comfortable. Make a mental note of how you are feeling and what your body is telling you about the situation. As the interview progresses, what is your body sensing and feeling? Are you suddenly feeling nervous, experiencing sweaty palms or fidgeting with your hands? Maybe you're at a loss for words at that moment, and you recognize that this is not your typical behavior. Or, perhaps you are more familiar with the fight or flight instinct that kicks in when your body responds to a perceived threat.

In other words, human emotion can lead to reactions before thinking, as time is of the essence in a response. A reactive response, which is your body speaking to you through your emotions, can lead to undesired results. The more you practice going with your gut, the more you are learning to use your instinct. Another example can be in social situations. Feeling uncomfortable in a large social setting might be overwhelming for some and exhilarating for others. Perhaps, the first day on the job can feel overwhelming. This is an opportunity to take mental notes and notice what your body is telling you.

Alternatively, when you feel exhilarated about something, your body is also providing feedback. This is your body instinct giving information and knowledge about you. The more you listen to the messages your body sends, the more you are learning your instinct. Like anything in life, with practice you can achieve better results.

Act now and make a list of the times you trusted your gut. If you can't immediately come up with a list, take time to reflect. Ask yourself, when did I trust my gut? What was the situation? What was the result? You may find that by doing this exercise, you will discover that you've made the right choice by going with your gut. By continually practicing going with your gut, you'll get better at doing what's right for *you*. As your life unfolds in different areas such as career, family and social situations, your instincts will develop, and you'll realize you've had these gut instincts before, but they're much stronger now. With time, your instincts will get sharper and more perceptive and as a result, will create a positive feedback loop. This positive feedback loop helps support, build and strengthen your self-confidence, which is a requirement for leading an empowered lifestyle.

Have you ever shared a *big* dream or goal with anyone? I mean an outrageous dream or goal, only to have it shot down because in other people's minds it was "too lofty or impossible." Learning with whom to share your lofty dreams and goals is another essential piece of the self-empowerment puzzle. Why do I mention this?

Your lofty dreams and goals are yours and no one else's. The advent of technology has transformed our lives in many positive aspects. Today, there are many social media programs and software applications encouraging us to share everything about our lives. It is not my intent to discourage anyone from sharing anything you choose to share. My point is for you to understand the concept of self-preservation as it relates to your dreams and goals. It is best to share your dreams and goals with like-minded people. Seek out people or a mentor who will encourage and support you in achieving your heart's desire.

When you share your aspirations with like-minded people, they will provide guidance and can assist in making you accountable. When you feel accountable, you can bet your overall commitment and involvement in that project will be higher. Follow up conversations with them will aid in the efforts to focus and clarify your intentions. Additionally, they can help you measure your progress and provide motivation when needed. From time to time, all of us can benefit from an extra dose of motivation. Ultimately, as you grow and develop in life, remember that whatever it is you choose for your career, *the goal is not to be free from work but to be free to find meaning in your work.*

I heard an interview where Mark Cuban, self-made billionaire and owner of the Dallas Mavericks, was recently asked what he considered are rules for success. I certainly agree with him and share them for *your* journey to *success*!

1. There simply are *no short-cuts* in life! Only you can find the solutions to the challenges you will face.
2. If there is one thing you can control in your life, it's the *effort* you put into it. The effort you put in will determine the outcome; however,

sometimes that effort does not result in the intended outcome. Disappointments are a fact of life and can teach us powerful lessons.

3. How do you *define success*? Is it about money? Is it happiness? Is it finding your passion? All of these can be defined as success.

Final Thoughts on Self-Empowerment

- Choose to be responsible for your life.

- Consider every set back as a set-up for success.

- Learn to know, understand and trust yourself.

- Expand your vocabulary; use powerful, dynamic word choices.

- Be authentic, honest, and believe in yourself.

- Take action to increase your self-confidence, no matter how small.

- Learn to see things from the other person's perspective.

- Create and develop good habits for your life.

- Resist the habit of comparing yourself to others.

- "If you change the way you look at things, the things you look at change." Dr. Wayne Dyer

- Reflect often on your own set of unique talents and gifts.

- Forgive yourself often and appreciate your accomplishments.
- Find a mentor for guidance, encouragement and motivation.
- Listen to your gut; your instincts can only be developed by you.
- "If at first you don't succeed, then try, try again!" Thomas H. Palmer
- You never fail until you give up!

Believe in yourself and remember **impatience guarantees defeat!** What's ahead is all that matters . . . The best is still yet to come. So, trust in your faith, and keep looking forward to your new beginnings.

Lastly, on a personal note and based on my own experiences, I believe there is a divine life force that guides us all. For me, that divine life force and spiritual belief system is the spirit energy of God. There was a time when I turned away from this enlightening energy force without realizing it. Earlier in my life, I was briefly married to someone who did not believe in a higher power and over the eight years we were together, my Christian faith and trust gradually diminished.

Looking back, I realize there were many lessons learned during that timeframe. For me, these times were filled with many challenges and struggles, both personally and professionally. One early spring morning, I was suddenly awakened, and as I sat up in my bed, the clear image of Jesus Christ, the Son of God was before me. What I heard *Him* say to me was, I have always been by your side, and *you* are the one who walked away. These powerful words and his image have never left me.

From that day forward, I *chose* to rebuild my trust and faith in God which took some time to develop. Now, I have a solid internal knowing, trust and belief that God's spirit is always with me and that no matter what the circumstance, I am being guided by *Him*. Life has a way of throwing us many curve balls, and we don't even realize it.

Whatever your religious background or spiritual belief system, remember that it is always your choice to live your life with free will.

It is always your choice.

References

Chapter 1

Dr. Marty Nemko on What Colleges and Graduate Schools Don't Want You to Know:

www.YouTube.com/watch?v=xp6VR6tq9k4

Chapter 3

Action Verbs:

http://career.opcd.wfu.edu/files/2011/05/Action-Verbs-for-Resumes.pdf

Chapter 4

Behavioral Questions:

https://www.thebalance.com/behavioral-job-interview-questions-2059620

Chapter 5

Hard Skills:

http://www.investopedia.com/terms/h/hard-skills.asp

Chapter 6

Budgeting Time:

http://www.cegeon.com/plain_printable_calendar.pdf

Chapter 7

Credit Scores:

https://www.experian.com/blogs/ask-experian/credit-education/score-basics/what-is-a-good-credit-score/

Chapter 8

Apprenticeships:

http://www.fldoe.org/core/fileparse.php/3/urlt/general
-apprenticeship-information.pdf

https://www.dol.gov/apprenticeship/

https://doleta.gov/oa/stateoffices.cfm#GA

https://doleta.gov/OA/regdirlist.cfm

https://www.careeronestop.org/

Contact Information

To contact Carmen Topper, please email:
relevantlifeskills@gmail.com

About the Author

Carmen is a passionate faith filled counselor and educator at heart with a master's degree in counseling. She earned her MS from Barry University, which is accredited by the Council for Accreditation of Counseling & Related Educational Programs (CACREP). Her genuine interest and compassion inspire people to understand that no matter what happens in life, with trust, faith, determination and perseverance, anything is possible.

Carmen gained a wealth of knowledge and wisdom while following a non-traditional career path in aviation, education, financial markets, media advertising, NYC real estate and the pulp and paper industry. While living in NYC and changing her career direction several times, she learned how to distinguish herself from other applicants and landed the prized jobs. From writing resumes with no guidance or direction, to randomly choosing roommates, she learned the hard way what not to do. Carmen has the ability to see the whole picture and inspires people to view things from a different perspective, enabling personal growth and development.